# DIANA

## QUEEN OF STYLE

# DIANA

## QUEEN OF STYLE

Jackie Modlinger

Foreword by
Zandra Rhodes

COURAGE
BOOKS
AN IMPRINT OF RUNNING PRESS
PHILADELPHIA • LONDON

Library of Congress Cataloging-in-Publication Number 97-76133

ISBN 0-7624-0405-1

Copyright © Jackie Modlinger 1998

The right of Jackie Modlinger to be identified as the author of this book has been asserted by her in accordance with the Copyright, Designs, and Patents Act, 1998.

This book was produced by CLB International, Godalming, Surrey, U.K.

Commissioning editor: Jane Alexander
Production: Graeme Proctor, Neil Randles

Produced for Quadrillion Publishing Ltd by
The Design Revolution, Brighton
Editor: Ian Whitelaw
Design: Fiona Roberts

Commissioned photography: Neil Sutherland and Ben Costa
Picture research: Christine Cornick

5107

Cover Photo Credits:
Front cover: Lord Snowdon (Camera Press)
Back cover: Jim Bennett (Alpha)
Back cover, bottom: Chancellor (Alpha)
Sketch: David Sassoon
Back flap: John Swannell

Published by Courage Books, an imprint of Running Press Book Publishers
125 South Twenty-second Street, Philadelphia, Pennsylvania 19103-4399
This book may be ordered by mail from the publisher.
*But try your bookstore first!*

**DEDICATION**
In loving memory of my parents Alex and Stella Modlinger,
and my grandmother Sali Wolf

# Contents

# Foreword BY ZANDRA RHODES

LADY DIANA SPENCER could have chosen to remain a Sloane Ranger, but that was not to be her destiny. Despite being so young and uninformed, or perhaps because of it, she was the one who dared, and she embarked on a huge and unimaginable adventure.

This is the story of the first royal superstar model, a beautiful woman who lived her remarkable life not on the catwalks of Paris, Milan, or London, but upon the world stage, in high society, but also among the people.

Rarely, if ever, are there pictures that show the creation of a superstar, but in Diana's case the eyes, and the lenses, of the world were on her from the moment she entered the royal arena. The pictures are here, carefully chosen, and they illustrate an unfolding transformation, one that took place so gradually that neither the Royal Family nor the watching public was aware of it.

In *Diana: Queen of Style,* the Princess of Wales' look and style are scrutinized in meticulous detail, as she blossoms from a classic English rose into an international beauty. Jackie Modlinger offers us a brilliant analysis of Diana's impact on the fashion world, and a wonderful account of a woman who, behind the scenes, dares to develop her character and her own distinctive dress sense.

This book is also a revelation, as well as a record for posterity, of the contribution made by the cutting-edge fashion designers, hairdressers, and milliners, in Britain and around the world. It shows how they responded to the challenge of dressing the world's most photographed woman, and how well they accomplished the task.

Through personal interviews with the fashion designers that knew and loved the Princess of Wales, Jackie captures the essense of what it was like to be part of the most exciting fashion story ever.

Setting the scene from the point of view of fashion, she recounts the milestones on the Princess' journey, and explains how so few of the designers who shared some of that journey traveled the full distance with the Princess. Diana was on a jet plane speeding ahead of them.

Only time will tell how we will remember this beautiful English woman who captured the world – a charismatic, compassionate, fairytale princess. This book captures her story, and shows us who she was.

ornamental
stitching to
hide pads.

dyed pink
toothstrip.

12

10

9

sequins
with pink
Rhinestones
in centre.

Detail of pleats on bodice
caught down with sequins & beads.

Cuff detail showing edge of cuff
hand whipped & finished with
alternate pearls & pink rhinestones.

Edge of bodice front & back

Zandra Rhodes
Style 85/113

**BRIGHTER THAN LIFE** *(left)* Painted by Zandra in her flamboyant and colorful style, this watercolor sketch shows the dress that she designed for Diana for a Birthright Benefit at the London Palladium. The white silk chiffon dress is printed in Edwardian style, with buttons and bows, and the draped skirt is edged in alternate pink glass beads and simulated pearls. The painting appeared in the Christie's catalogue for the auction of the Princess of Wales' dresses.

*Photograph of Zandra Rhodes*
*(opposite) by Robyn Beeche*

# chapter one
# the early years

"I had one long dress, one silk shirt,
one smart pair of shoes, and that was it.
Suddenly my mother and I had
to buy six of everything."

LADY DIANA SPENCER ON "E" (ENGAGEMENT) DAY

# Once Upon a Time...

THE YOUNG ROMANTIC *(above)* Lady Diana Spencer in a naive-knit, reindeer-patterned cardigan, white piecrust-frilled cotton shirt with black velvet ribbon tie, and gray pinstripe pencil skirt, pictured leaving her flat in Coleherne Court in early 1981.

## "I need beautiful clothes for someone very important."

"BEA" MILLER, *VOGUE* EDITOR

SEEN IN GREEN *(previous page)* Worn over a crisp white ruff-collared blouse, this green raw silk suit with pintucked jacket detail, ball buttons, contrast blue circles on sleeves and wrist, matching belt, and pleated skirt, was first seen on a visit to Broadlands, home of the late Lord Mountbatten, in May 1981.

A FLASHBACK TO A DAY in the late summer of 1980 sees history in the making. The caption may well have read "Here's looking at you, kid," as budding English rose, 19-year-old Lady Diana Spencer, a nursery school assistant at Young England in London's Pimlico, is captured on camera by a posse of press photographers, with her two small charges in tow.

This is an image that will prove seminal, for Diana is the girl destined to be Prince Charles' bride, the future Princess of Wales.

"Lady Di," as she came to be dubbed, is wearing a sheer, sprigged, mid-length voile skirt by Laura Ashley, paired with lilac lambswool slipover and shirt. There is nothing very remarkable in any of this, except that the picture just happens to be back-lit, revealing the leggy silhouette of a then rather chubby-looking Lady Di, an image that was not totally "comme-il-faut" for a would-be princess.

Nevertheless, revealing though the skirt may be, it is in no way provocative. Indeed, it's rather endearing in its innocence. The young nursery school helper looks somewhat coy and embarrassed, and her expression is one that will earn her the title of "Shy Di." Rumor has it that the pictures that appeared in the press the following day made Lady Diana cry.

They also marked the unveiling of a fashion fairy tale. From that day onward, for 16 years, the Di-spies would be besotted by Diana, who was to make the quantum leap from super-Sloane [the English version of trend-setting "preppy"] to megastar, and become the world's most watched and photographed woman.

Given time, the butterfly would emerge from her chrysalis, spread her wings, and become the most celebrated Supermodel of them all; a fashion and style icon whose influence was to span one-and-a-half decades. The fashpack would dub Diana the POW (short for Princess of Wales or, to some, the Prisoner of Wales), and she would emerge as the Fairy Godmother of British fashion.

Here, at last, was the perfect royal clotheshorse on which to hang fashion stories. Diana's was a look that was to spawn many a clone, shape the careers of a clutch of British designers, and alter the course of British fashion. In time she was even to change the course of the monarchy itself.

At first, her style is Sloaney, girly, and unsophisticated; her labels are unpretentious like those of her flatmates in her London Coleherne Court apartment. She shops at Laura Ashley, Benetton, and Inca, reserving Harrods and Harvey "Nicks" for special occasions.

Her wardrobe staples are piecrust-frilled blouses, naively patterned knobbly sweaters, eclectic Peruvian knits, classic angora or Shetland cardigans, safe mid-calf- length skirts, and knickerbockers. Accessories are pearls and velvet chokers, provençal-print bags, and flat practical pumps. By night, a casual Loden coat skims a long evening dress.

The eyes of the world are riveted on Lady Diana Spencer; the prying lens never leaves her; there is growing speculation that she is the one who is destined to be Queen of England.

"Long before we got to know her officially," remembers Robina Ziff, " ... she came to our Knightsbridge shop in a green Loden coat and tried on an evening dress—in apple-green tulle by Nettie Vogues (they're no longer in business). It was around $700-750. She really liked it but she said: 'I must ask Daddy, because it's awfully expensive!' I'll always remember that. Shortly afterward, they announced the engagement."

Meanwhile, there are whispers up at glossy British *Vogue*. Designers such as David Sassoon, Gina Fratini, and a virtually unknown couple, the Emanuels, are asked to submit pretty, frilly blouses for a feature on "English roses." *Vogue* Editor Beatrix (a.k.a. "Bea") Miller calls Argentinean fashion guru Roberto Devorik, of Regine in London's Bond Street, with the request: "I need beautiful clothes for someone very important." The VIP was Lady Diana Spencer.

**INNOCENCE IS THIS** *(left)* The alarm bell, or rather wedding bell, tolled with that diaphanous voile skirt that trailblazed the fairy tale. The famous back-lit shot of Shy Di with her two small charges was taken in all innocence. With her mid-calf length sheer Laura Ashley printed voile skirt, lilac shirt, and V-necked Benetton slipover, Diana epitomizes the quintessential, uncontrived English Sloane style of her generation.

**SHORT OVER LONG** *(above)* Conspicuous by its absence in the Super-Sloane's wardrobe, at this stage, was an evening coat. Meanwhile, Lady Di has to make do with wearing her practical all-purpose Loden coat as coverall the clock round— even skimming a long evening dress.

The February 1981 issue of *Vogue* had to go to press a couple of months in advance, and even with inside knowledge of the pending engagement between Prince Charles and Lady Diana, the magazine could not break the story until it became official. So they did the next best thing, hinting at it with a feature that, with careful reading between the lines, said it all.

Photographed by Lord Snowdon, and subtly veiled under the title "Portrait Portfolio," was a six-page feature on English roses, the lead spread being "Lady Diana Spencer, 19, youngest daughter of the Earl Spencer and the Hon. Mrs Peter Shand Kydd."

Lady Diana was photographed looking magical in a cropped shot of a cream organdie and lace dress by Gina Fratini and a pink chiffon blouse by the Emanuels. The text was extremely cleverly worded and read, "The camera has a unique capacity to conserve a moment of time. A portrait photograph by definition possesses immediacy and believability. The photographed face is the face of that moment." Those cryptic words hinted at an exciting secret. "Duch" (short for Duchess)—the Spencer's family nickname for Diana—was poised to become a princess-in-waiting.

Within days, the engagement was official. February 16, 1981, was E-Day, confirming that Lady Diana Spencer was indeed "The One." To mark her engagement, she wore a rather mumsy, forgettable royal blue crêpe suit with scalloped jacket detail, and a bird-print blouse, bought off-the-peg at Harrods for $530 on her mother's account. The Bellville-Sassoon sailor suit she chose for her official engagement picture with Her Majesty The Queen was a decided improvement, being younger, fresher, and much more in keeping with her personality.

## "The photographed face is the face of the moment."

*VOGUE*, FEBRUARY 1981

**COVER-GIRL INCARNATE** *(left)* Flashback to the February 1981 issue of the fashion bible, *Vogue*. Captured in camera by Lord Snowdon on the opening spread of a six-page story on English roses, Lady Diana Spencer wears a blush-pink, ruffled chiffon blouse paired with a taffeta skirt with satin ribbons by the Emanuels, who were to make the wedding dress. In six months' time, a far cry from being subtly concealed between the glossy sheets, *Vogue* would feature this same English rose as their cover girl.

Margaret Boyton, who works in the separates department of Fenwick of Bond Street, a favorite haunt in the early Lady Di days, recalls the Super-Sloane coming in to the store during the engagement period. "She went for coffee with friends, having just admired a pair of black velvet knickerbockers that had been put out. Lady Di couldn't resist them, and, on the way out, she had to buy them."

Almost 13 years younger than Charles, her husband-to-be (whom she had met at a shooting party three years' earlier), "Shy Di" was perfect Pygmalion material. Anna Harvey, senior fashion editor at *Vogue*, was to become her designated "Professor Higgins."

From the point of view of fashion, credit for the engagement, the run-up to the wedding, and the wedding of the century must go to the Emanuels and to David Sassoon.

"Anna Harvey of *Vogue* called us—Lord Snowdon was doing a portrait of 'someone very famous'— did we have something high-necked?" remembers Liz Emanuel.

**SAILOR-GIRL STYLE** *(above)* Following a visit to Cheltenham on March 27, 1981, Diana poses for her official engagement picture with Her Majesty The Queen and her fiancé. To mark the occasion, Diana wears a patriotic navy wool crêpe suit paired with a white top-stitched sailor blouse with red satin bow trim. A single-strand pearl necklace and navy clutchbag provide the finishing touches.

> "She was fresh, with wonderful eyes."

DAVID EMANUEL

"We sent in a pale pink chiffon blouse and a pink taffeta ballerina skirt," adds David Emanuel. "It was only afterward that we found out that it was for Diana. She loved the blouse, was told it was ours, and phoned up to tell us that she wanted to see what else we were doing."

"I'll never forget when that buzzer went and she walked up the stairs; at the time her face was all over the newspapers and there was all the speculation," recalls Liz.

"She was fresh, with beautiful skin, and clear, sparkling blue eyes, and fun; a bit leggy and gawky, because she was young," remembers David.

"She had huge charisma; she was very beautiful in a very Sloaney style, still quite full-faced, tall, fresh-faced, and kind; easy and informal, which was a surprise—you'd think that she would be a bit guarded, yet she was so very open and warm; unsure of herself, though, as far as clothes were concerned," says Liz of Lady Di.

**DIANA'S DEBUT *VOGUE* COVER** (right)
Lady Diana Spencer was just married as the August issue of *Vogue* hit the newsstands. Shot by Lord Snowdon, this was the first of several cover shots for the magazine Diana would pose for.

**E-DAY OUTFIT** *(top)* The sapphire-blue three-piece suit with a scalloped, self-belted jacket and dowdy, mid-length skirt, and the tie-necked bluebird print blouse were purchased at Harrods.

**DEMURE DÉCOLLETAGE** *(above)* Puff sleeves and rustling taffeta, essential ingredients in an evening dress at the time, were encapsulated in this long, romantic dress designed by Graham Wren for Nettie Vogues.

**OFF-DUTY DI** *(left)* Lady Di relaxes in the country in an eclectic fuchsia V-necked sweater from Inca, the London Peruviana shop, paired with cord knickerbockers and Hunter Wellingtons.

## "All the world loves a makeover."

LIZ EMANUEL

**DI BY NIGHT IN "THAT DRESS"** *(above)* Following their engagement announcement of February 24, March 9 saw the couple at their first formal evening "do," held at Goldsmith's Hall in the City of London. *Princess Grace of Monaco was the celebrity guest.*

**THAT DRESS** *(right)* A full-length view of the famous black frilled, strapless taffeta dress, the result of the working sketch *(left)*. Although the dress was worn in all innocence, its décolletage and bareness were deemed daring. The press and photographers had a field day.

**DEBUT PREMIER** *(far left)* David Sassoon fitted Diana for her first James Bond premier, *For Your Eyes Only*, in June 1981. She needn't have worried about "falling out of it, like the last one" (the Emanuels' black dress)—Sassoon had been dressing royal ladies for long enough to know the score and avoid a repeat performance.

**LOCAL HEROINE** *(left)* In her favorite hot spots—Jasper Conran's red and white V-necked polka dot jacket, cinched with a wide leather belt worn over a white ruffled blouse and solid red skirt —Diana visits Tetbury, England, in March 1981.

"The engagement blouse, the black taffeta dress, and the wedding dress are the most significant pieces that we made for her," insists David. The daringly décolleté taffeta dress that Diana wore to her first official public engagement with Prince Charles was dynamite, giving a first glimpse of her cover-girl quality. "It was just a simple dress that I had hanging in the show-room, and it had actually been worn once by Liza Goddard [British TV personality]. Lady Diana asked for something off-the-peg; she needed it quickly and there was no time to make a dress from scratch," recalls Liz.

"She looked through the clothes, and on a second visit we were working on the black taffeta. We showed it to her, she tried it on, and she looked sensational," says David. "I need something formal," she said. "It couldn't be more so," he told her. Diana fell in love with the black dress.

"We couldn't have envisaged the impact of seeing her in something so curvaceous and glamorous; for us, it was just a black dress; we were over-whelmed by the impact it made when she stepped out of the limo, revealing all that cleavage. It knocked the Budget off the front page of every newspaper," chortles Liz, still relishing the thought.

David remembers: "Everyone was craning over the balcony shooting down and Trevor McDonald [Britain's most popular anchorman] said, 'Let's show that again on '*News at Ten*.' The action replay was such a shock. Lady Di had only ever been seen in sweaters and pearls—a teenager—and now–wow! There was this glamorous young woman, who had a great figure."

"I think that is what contributed toward the media interest ... that one night showed this incredible trans-formation – all the world loves a makeover, and Lady Di suddenly went from being a somewhat dumpy nursery-school helper in frilly blouses to a young, sexy rose in full bloom," enthuses Liz.

By most standards, the black taffeta was a fairly conventional dress, and one that has since been likened to a similar style worn by the Queen herself more than 30 years earlier. It was simply the bare shoulders and décolletage that caused such a furore among the press and the public.

Rumor has it that the Queen Mother gave Diana a dressing-down over the taffeta number the following morning. Whether this is true or not, Diana certainly took the criticism on board, for when David Sassoon was making her a similar long red and gold spotted evening dress, she begged: "Please make sure that you don't make me look as if I'm falling out of it, like the last one!"

# The Wedding Dress

CLOSE-UP (above) The bodice of the wedding dress of the century. The Emanuels designed a fairy-tale dress—a dramatic, romantic design in ivory pure silk taffeta overlaid, with pearl-encrusted lace, full-blown sleeves caught with bows at the elbow, and a ruffled décolleté neckline.

THE BIG QUESTION was, "Who would get the dream commission—the wedding dress?" Gina Fratini, whose white, draped sari-silk dress was to open the Christie's auction of Princess Diana's dresses, was a contender. "I was sad that I didn't get the wedding dress; everyone expected me to; I would have loved to have done it, and I think that I would have done it well ... I certainly would have known what fabric would crease or not."

The Emanuels were chosen to do the dress as the result of a com-

> ## "The process of designing her dress was very relaxed and informal."
>
> LIZ EMANUEL

petition in *Vogue*. Liz remembers: "A number of designers were invited to submit ideas for wedding dresses; I remember that ours was in cream— I think that Anna Harvey at *Vogue* still has it. That was the initial link with the Princess and a way of seeing what designers might do for her, but we had built up our own relationship with her; she liked the privacy of our place, the fact that you had to ring the doorbell to gain entry; that we were really casual, just let her look around; I think that's probably why she got on so well with us."

David recalls: "So far as the dress was concerned, it was a three-way conversation, between Diana, Elizabeth, and myself. We had assumed that there would be protocol and guidelines—after all, this was supposed to be the biggest wedding of the century. Yet there were no guidelines. After the initial announcement that 'the unknown Emanuels' had been chosen to make the wedding gown, at the end of that week, the Press Officer, Michael Shea, rang us up and just said, 'Oh, marvelous – whatever you're doing, just keep on doing it.'"

The dress took four months to make from the date of the commission. "We closed our business from the time of the announcement to the wedding day. There were so many people trying to get into the place ... seamstresses were offered suitcases of money; people raided the rubbish-bins; we'd wrap up scraps of fabric and burn them ... it was exciting, but when Lady Diana came, it was even more so... she was so enthusiastic and appreciative – you got a tremendous buzz from it.

"Inspiration for the wedding dress came from part of an existing collection—Lady Diana saw a sample and asked for her bridal gown to be based on it—we did, in fact, make it very different—she tried on everything in our studio, and she really, really liked that one. We made up an alternative, just in case. I tried to cover every eventuality – we even made up an overskirt in case the bride spilt

THE PRINCESS IN HER DRESS (right) A full-length portrait of the newly wed Princess of Wales in her spectacular wedding dress. It had a sweep of costume drama to it, which was very Emanuel. "She'd seen something similar on the rails, tried on all the shapes, but settled for this one because it had a really pretty neckline," remembers Liz.

coffee over it during the wedding breakfast. We were really over-the-top careful. We absolutely appreciated this amazing honor that was being given to us as designers," recalls Liz.

Everything has to be viewed in its context. "I would never design a dress like that now," says Liz, "but at the time it was great. I was upset by that remark 'Oh I hope that the moths get it' that she is supposed to have made. I truly believe that the Princess liked the dress, as she sat for her portrait in it."

SHILTON'S SLIPPER (above) Diana, a real-life Cinderella married her fella' in a stylish marriage that was orchestrated right down to the foot-finish —to complement her dress, shoemaker Clive Shilton made her a pair of silk slippers with a heart motif composed of pearls and sequins.

Diana at that formative time, very lucky indeed. Nobody can take that away from us."

"Diana was the kind of woman whom we wanted to dress—beautiful, famous, loved by the public. She was a trend-setter, idolized and cloned by everybody. I don't think that I can name one person who has ever enjoyed so much limelight or exposure," believes David.

"Meeting the Princess did change our life—it was a real turning-point. Our career took off and changed things forever. My life is quite a parallel with hers—Charles is a Scorpio; we

"We made the toile (linen fitting) straight away; we did some research and joked about the train—should we make it detachable or not? We thought about sitting down for the wedding breakfast and wondered how long we should make it. The longest train on record was 20 feet. 'Yes, let's make it bigger', we thought. Like 25 feet long! When we came to fit it, we realized that we didn't have sufficient room to display a train that long. 'We'll have to come over to you, Ma'am,' we told Diana, 'to the palace. We'll bring the toile because we need to splay it out.'

"We jumped into a cab, went to St. Paul's, measured the width of the aisle, so that we knew what we had to play

with, took the toile skirt, and went to BP. None of the bedrooms there was big enough, so the only option was the hall—we had to get rid of all those people, footmen and all. So I cleared the place, which was not easy, as everyone wanted to watch, but I had sworn to keep the dress a secret, so I made them leave.

"They thought that I was mad at the time. Imagine! We sealed off one entire floor of Buckingham Palace and locked the door at each end. I got the shears, folded the train in half, and cut a curve. We were all giggling away and that was it. Outside, people started to knock, so Diana jumped out of the dress; we folded it up in a

big sheet and opened the doors. When I think back on it, I can't believe it—the fact that we just siphoned off an entire floor of the palace," remembers David.

"In the early days," recalls Liz, "it was part of the adventure; we were very lucky to have met and worked for

## "Meeting the Princess changed our life ... our career took off and it changed things forever."

LIZ EMANUEL

both married, had two children, and split from our husbands," says Liz.

"In the run-up to the wedding, Lady Di lost loads of weight," she confirms. "Nina, the fitter, was constantly taking in the wedding dress, which was designed when we first met her. She was kind of busty, so it

**THE NEWLY WEDS** *(left)* On the steps of St. Paul's Cathedral. Her "something old" was the Carrickmackross lace —an heirloom from Queen Mary—that the Emanuels had dyed a little lighter to match the dress. Her "something blue" was a tiny bow, stitched into the waistband. She had "borrowed" the family heirlooms—the Spencer tiara and her mother's diamond earrings—and her good-luck charm was a miniscule gold and diamond horseshoe hidden in the folds of the taffeta.

**FAIRY-TALE TWOSOME** *(below left)* A close-up of the Prince and his bride. The Princess of Wales wears the Spencer family tiara falling onto a veil of silk tulle with hand-embroidered mother-of-pearl sequins spanning the length of the train.

**THE LONGEST TRAIN** *(far left)* Exit lines were a trademark touch that came to be synonymous with the Princess of Wales, who started as she meant to go on. The first and finest example of this trait was the 25 foot train on her wedding dress, the longest royal train to date.

was created to show a bit of cleavage, but by the time of the final fitting, she had lost a serious amount of weight—her waist measurement went from 27 or 28 down to just 23inches.

"The wedding itself was an awesome occasion," continues Liz. "The cathedral so big, getting Diana right, TV being on, and us being inside seeing the crowds on the screen and hearing them outside St. Paul's; us having that secret knowledge of what the dress was going to look like, my mother backstage putting the finishing touches to the veil—it was such an extraordinary time."

The wedding took place on July 29, 1981, and after Diana had left Buckingham Palace in her fairy-tale carriage, she actually took the trouble to ring the Emanuels—"I just wanted to say thank-you for making me such a wonderful dress." This was always Diana's style.

"She would always say 'thank you' in person and take the time to write. She was one of those people for whom, however heavy one's schedule, if she asked 'could you do this... ?', one would say 'of course'," remembers David affectionately.

*Vogue*'s August issue contained the Snowdon portraits, shot in advance, and showed the new Princess as Cover Girl in a cropped headshot, wearing a diamond parure. The inside spread featured Prince Charles and the then Lady Diana Spencer together, the Prince in full naval regalia; Lady Diana was wearing a long, green taffeta ballgown by David Sassoon, with bow-trimmed puff sleeves and a décolleté neckline, falling onto a full, whooshy skirt.

In the same August issue, Elizabeth Longford wrote in a piece on royal weddings: "The wedding of the century is now part of history, and, like all true history, it will leave its mark on the future. The marriage of Prince Charles and Lady Diana Spencer shows the British Monarchy edging away from the extremes of pomp and circumstance toward the intimacy of a family occasion."

How very prophetic she was.

FEW DESIGNERS CAN boast a track-record of dressing royal women for four decades. David Sassoon is one. "Over the years, I have dressed all of them—Princess Anne, Princess Margaret, Princess Michael (he made her wedding dress), Princess Alexandra and Fergie," says the designer.

"In her heyday, Princess Margaret enjoyed the same kind of media attention as Princess Diana; she was very glamorous in the sixties, the Liz Taylor of the royals," he believes. "But that was very formal dressing. When Princess Diana stepped in, she changed the rules; she lightened up the whole fashion business," says David. "She was more fun to dress than Margaret—so star-ish, and she had such a divine figure," he enthuses.

# David SASSOON

**THE ANDY-PANDY SUIT** *(above)* Sassoon made Diana's first Ascot outfit for June 1981—a three-piece suit comprising candy-striped organza blouse paired with jerkin-jacket and slim-line skirt.

"She changed the guidelines, broke the rules; Diana was the first of the royals to wear trousers.

"We were one of the first designers she ever went to, apart from the Emanuels. We had a secret code in the press book—'Miss Buckingham'," he recalls. "Lady Diana Spencer was first introduced to me by her mother, Mrs. Shand Kydd, a client of mine," says Sassoon, who remembers Diana as "this gauche, shy young girl, who had this habit of always tilting her head."

At one time, Shy Di was, says the designer, "a Sloane Ranger, with a penchant for romantic dressing, who favored the full-skirted, strapless taffeta styles inspired by the grand couture of the time. The trademark Sloane signatures—the puritanical and

dandy touches—were left over from her flat-sharing days. Then she got dressed up," he recalls.

Sassoon was responsible for some 60 designs during Diana's lifetime, and many were memorable milestones. The first was the navy wool-crêpe sailor-suit for Lady Diana Spencer's official engagement picture with the Queen. He also made her "going-away" outfit, a two-piece in cantaloupe melon-colored wild silk with her favorite piecrust-frilled collar and cuffs.

"By the time we had made the "going-away" outfit, I adored her. We used to sit on the floor, laugh and have coffee together, but it was after she chose the white/gold Empire-line dress for the premier of a play with Liz Taylor that she changed completely

**PURITAN PRINCESS** *(above)* A favorite white, lace blouse in the New Romantic style worn under a black wool crêpe suit, was worn for the Remembrance Day Service in November 1981.

and became HRH," recalls David. "She seemed to become aware for the first time ever that she was now a royal princess and that, as such, it was no longer seemly to sit on the floor and be called 'Diana.'"

For her visit to the 'Splendours of The Gonzaga' exhibition at London's Victoria and Albert Museum in November 1981, Sassoon made the Princess a dream of a dress—hand-painted, embroidered chiffon, off-the-shoulder, it fell onto a full-skirted crinoline skirt. It was slotted with baby-blue satin ribbon, echoed in the

**WAITING FOR HARRY** *(above)* Prettily pregnant in a long ivory Empire-line chiffon evening dress.

**GONZAGA GOWN** *(left and above)* Sassoon's original working drawing for the romantic "Gonzaga" dress. "That dress was every child's vision of a real-life princess, and replica dolls were made featuring this particular design," says David Sassoon of the gown—a hand-painted, off-the-shoulder satin ribbon-slotted, waist-sashed long chiffon dress with crinoline skirt.

sashed waist. "Children wrote to me," remembers Sassoon. "That particular dress epitomized every child's version of a fairy-tale princess."

At Christie's auction in 1997, Lot No. 77—"a cherubic black and gold draped evening dress with jeweled straps" – went under the hammer for $23,000 and was bought by *Paris Match* for a competition. This was the last dress that David and his partner Lorcan Mullany made for the Princess.

At Christie's reception in London, David asked Diana what she had done with the going-away outfit? "I'm hanging on to it," she replied. And then she went away, forever.

# chapter two
# search for a style

"The image I have of her has
always been one of tenderness,
color, and joie-de-vivre."

KENZO TAKADA

# Great Expectations . . .

**THE WHITE THING** *(above)* A double-breasted, white cashmere coat provides the perfect foil for a newly acquired honeymoon tan. This coat, from Courtenay House in Brook Street, London, was doubtless purchased en route to one of the numerous fittings at the Emanuels' studio.

## "I like seeing a lady well dressed."

PRINCE CHARLES

**DOWN BY THE RIVERSIDE** *(previous page)* For the famous photo-call on the banks of the River Dee, the new wife of Windsor wore a checked Harris tweed suit with blouson-style jacket and mid-calf length skirt. "I decided on the style," recalls designer Bill Pashley.

SO FAR, SO GOOD. Cinderella, a.k.a. Diana, has married her Prince Charming, and become a princess. After a stylish marriage, she has been swept away in a glass carriage. The people are enchanted with their beautiful new princess; her wedding has lent the country a whole new mood of romance and optimism. The future looks rosy.

Two of the most magical images of the Princess of Wales belong to the honeymoon period, an all-too-brief respite from public life. One is of Diana on the Royal Yacht *Britannia*. Looking incredibly happy, fresh, and girly, she is dressed in Kenzo's white, pintucked cotton puff-sleeved blouse with matching Bermudas; flat white sandals and a perky little natural straw bowler.

Paris-based Japanese designer, Kenzo Takada comments: "At the time of her marriage, she was very young, very natural, and romantic, which is how I like to think of my fashion. The image that I have of her has always been one of tenderness, color, and joie-de-vivre. I was always very touched when I happened to learn that the Princess of Wales was wearing my designs, and I think that they suited her very well, because they are free-spirited, as she is. She strongly wished to be her own woman, and to remain both natural and modern at the same time."

Although she was very much a woman of her time, the Princess would often dress too matronly for her age in the early years, doubtless because of her position and palace protocol. "In the beginning, a lot of the prints were too old and mumsy," comments designer Jan Vanvelden.

She tended to look her best "au naturel," her hair windswept, and dressed in the casual, sportswear-orientated styles she wore to polo matches at Windsor.

My all-time favorite picture is that of the Wales' photo call on August 19, 1981, on the banks of the River Dee. Di has that coy, endearing little-girl-lost-look. Although Diana would come to hate this royal retreat, at this moment she is very much in love. This image is not so much about fashion, but about her style.

Her highlights are blonder and she is much slimmer. The dogtooth-checked suit, with its blouson-style jacket and mid-length skirt with center-inverted pleat, is uninspired, yet suited to the setting. Made by her mother's designer, Bill Pashley, it now looks oversized on her.

The Prince likes his wife to sport bare, brown legs, and the Princess, despite the chill of Scotland's early autumn, is reluctant to conceal her newly tanned limbs. Her shy smile, and the throwaway way she wears the suit with flat ballerina pumps, make this a memorable moment.

Being a Di-Watcher on a national newspaper kept you on your toes. The back bench and the newsdesk were always on your case, hungry for the designer or source of Di's latest designs, and it was quite a coup at the time when I managed to get an exclusive center-spread interview with Bill Pashley, the man responsible for the tweed blouson suit.

"Battersea" (the location of his studio) Bill is a quiet Yorkshireman. He is the unsung hero of the early Diana days, the man who made the memorable Harris tweed blouson suit worn for the River Dee photocall.

I caught up with him again recently, and he remembered those heady days. "I think that I probably did her very first ballgown," recalls Pashley, who met Lady Diana just before the wedding, through her mother who was an existing client. He reckons he made about 25 pieces for the princess in total.

"She wanted some clothes that would be suitable for Scotland and I made her knicker-bockers, a Loden cape, that suit, and a cotton two-piece for the wedding rehearsal. I also made her two or three evening dresses, and a black velvet cape [everybody wanted a velvet evening cape at the time], the outfit where she rushed off in tears at the polo match, a red coat, and a brown flannel suit worn with a trilby to Sandown Races when she

**FLOWER POWER** *(left)* Leaving Southampton after the first leg of her honeymoon, spent at Broadlands like the Queen and the Duke of Edinburgh, the Princess wears a white silk façonné floral-print dress with a front-tying jacket by Donald Campbell, her Courtenay cashmere coat slung casually over her shoulders.

**ORIGINAL CONCEPTION** *(right)* Kenzo's sketch for the white cotton, balloon-sleeved blouse with pretty pintuckery detail and Bermudas she wore, teamed with with a natural straw cloche hat and flat tan sandals, on her honeymoon.

**A LITTLE KENZO** *(below)* Although the Princess wore quite a few of his designs, it was not until 1988 at Sydney Opera House that the Princess got to meet the Paris-based Japanese designer, who is pictured here greeting her. On that occasion, the Princess wore Bruce Oldfield's midnight-blue satin ensemble.

**BATHROBE COAT** *(right)* A blonde, camel-colored tweed belted coat by Caroline Charles, worn with white ruffled silk blouse. The velvet skullcap with a stalk and dotted veil, and with plumed cockade at the side, was designed by John Boyd.

**CELTIC CHIC** *(far right)* Wales' very own princess flies the home flag, deliberately mismatching a scarlet, fitted jacket and skimming bottle-green pleated skirt by Donald Campbell, worn with graphic lacquer-red, large-brimmed hat, with bow trim, by John Boyd.

was newly engaged in March 1981," recalls Pashley. "I only had a day to make it. I stopped just after the wedding – when she moved into the big time," he says modestly.

Pashley has always kept a very low profile. He is a graduate of the Royal College of Art (RCA), and a contemporary of David Sassoon. The two overlapped for two out of the three year course at the RCA, where Sassoon was a year ahead of Pashley, who had come south to attend this prestigious college, that was, at the time, Britain's only fashion university.

"It is all a long time ago; her mother still keeps in touch; I am still doing wedding dresses and the like.

"We were both (David Sassoon and I) invited to the wedding; we sat next to each other; I think that she must have done her homework."

At the time of the Dee shoot, Prince Charles certainly had a high opinion of his wife's dress sense. "You know, I like seeing a lady well-dressed.

It was one of the things I always noticed about her before we got married. She had, I thought, a very good sense of style and design." Diana certainly never failed to do credit to her husband and "The Firm."

Her first public tour was to Wales, where she wowed the Celts and lived up to her title. For Caernarfon she choose a red Donald Campbell fitted jacket with bottle-green pleated skirt, set off with a red saucer hat by milliner John Boyd. For Brecon, she opted for an elegant Jaeger maroon velvet suit, with contrast-braiding and a white ruffle blouse and triple-strand pearl choker, with a matching plumed baby bowler, again by John Boyd.

The familiar Loden coat that once partnered evening gowns in the flat-sharing Coleherne Court days was exchanged for a long black velvet fairy-tale cape with pastel-pink lining. Arabella Pollen's leather-trimmed windowpane checked tweed coat-dress and beret were perfect. Bella

**WALES REVISITED** *(above)* On another visit to Barmouth in November 1982, the Princess wore a long, tattersall checked tweed coat-dress with a gathered skirt and leather trim and buttons, set off with a matching leather-trimmed beret. The outfit hailed from a new design talent—Arabella Pollen.

**THE VELVET TOUCH** *(left)* At Brecon, Diana was seen in this eggplant velvet suit with contrasting black braid trim, looped ball buttons, and a gently gathered skirt, over her signature New Romantic-style cream ruffled blouse. The outfit, off-the-peg, by Jaeger, was set off by a matching plumed tricorne-style hat by John Boyd.

was a young designer, and she had a special empathy with Diana.

For her first State Opening of Parliament, on November 4, David Sassoon made the Princess a long white dress. He remembers: "She was so very excited about it—'It is the first time I have ever worn a long evening dress during the day,' she enthused.

"I had made that specially for her and she helped with the design—she was quite specific about it ... it was the only time that she really attempted to be very specific—she sent me this little drawing, a rough sketch, we had a discussion and adapted it from what she actually drew. I felt that it was too Elizabethan—she had the waist going into a dramatic point. She just fell in love with the chiffon fabric, and it was very pretty with embroidery—like trees bearing little pieces of fruit, little pearls and crystal pears dropping off the trees. But I have to say, we were never very happy with it," he admits.

That same evening, Diana wore what came to be dubbed Sassoon's "Gonzaga" dress to the Victoria and Albert Museum for the opening of the 'Splendours of the Gonzaga' exhibition. She looked sublime, like a fairy princess, in the be-ribboned organza confection, originally part of her trousseau.

Diana had had a long, hard day, and, at one point, she was caught cat-napping, her head tilted to one side. The reason for her uncontrollable tiredness soon became apparent. The next morning we learned the Princess was expecting her first child.

**BERET NICE** (left) Berets were one of the most suitable, most flattering hat shapes for the Princess. Graham Smith made some of her best, like this perky style in coral with contrast black binding and bow trim to match the suit by Bella Pollen.

**NIGHT FOR DAY** (far left) The Princess' first State Opening of Parliament. To mark the occasion, David Sassoon made her a long white V-necked dress with a Tudor-style pointed waistline and embroidered bell-shaped sleeves.

Although editors don't usually favor maternity features, because they don't make for great pictures, an avalanche of maternity fashion articles appeared in the press in the run-up to Prince William's birth. For once, this subject was seen in a fashionable light.

Diana is on record as saying: "Nobody told me that I would feel like this." Being dogged by morning sickness while still struggling with her new Royal role was doubly daunting.

Charles confided to a member of a BBC camera crew during an interview at Highgrove in December, "She's finding pregnancy harder work than expected." However, there was no better excuse for a completely new royal wardrobe.

"I hated the maternity period—it wasn't my strong point, and she wore terrible hats with the outfits," laments David Sassoon. "She had lots of maternity outfits from me, but I have

to say that those she wore at the beginning, when she was going to John Boyd (the milliner), were unfortunate," agrees Jan Vanvelden.

The milliner, dubbed "the wee Scotsman," received a lot of flak, and he was not best pleased with the way Diana wore his hats. "Just send the piece of fabric to the milliner," Diana would say. A swatch would simply be despatched, which is probably why the result was often so disappointing.

The Princess looked far younger when she stopped wearing so many hats, although berets, particularly those made to match outfits by Arabella Pollen and Bruce Oldfield, did suit her.

Plunged into pregnancy almost immediately following her marriage, the royal mother-to-be seemed eager to flaunt her condition and quickly moved into maternity clothes.

The day after the announcement, she wore a loose-fitting, red, multi-colored yoked coat with fringed trim and electric blue accessories. Because it was winter, Diana ordered a whole wardrobe of hot-bright, smock-style coats from designers Bellville-Sassoon,

**RED-LETTER-DAY** *(top)* Sassoon's red, multistriped loosely woven wool coat and a periwinkle blue John Boyd mini-bowler.

**PRETTY IN PEACH** *(above)* Silk maternity dress with tonal cardigan, at the Guards' Polo Club.

**POM-POMMERY** *(right)* The neckline and yoke of this fuchsia maternity coat featured pom-pom ties worn with a matching bowler.

**VELVET TRIM** *(far left)* Another maternity special from Sassoon—a coat in fir green with velvet trim on collar, cuffs, and arabesque frieze, with a matching boater-style hat with ribbon crown trim.

**EASY PIECES** *(left)* For playing the waiting game—a lipstick pink sweatshirt over a white shirt, paired with turquoise bermuda shorts.

**BEARING UP** *(bottom left)* The Princess makes a feature out of her "bump" with a fun koala-motifed Sloppy Joe sweater worn over red pants.

in fuchsia-pink or peacock with wide, ruffled puritan collars, yokes, braid trim, and pom-pom neckties, designed to detract from the baby-bulge. The most chic design of all was a fir-green coat with velvet arabesque appliqué.

The prettiest dress David made for her first pregnancy was a long, wine-colored Empire-line taffeta evening dress, embellished with contrasting white lace, worn to a London chartity event when she was three months pregnant.

As she blossomed, Diana looked best at informal occasions such as polo matches. For these she dressed in oversized sweaters worn over pedal-pushers or sporty dungarees. These were infinitely more flattering than the nondescript, tentlike dresses in green or blue spot-ways, often accompanied by cardigans, that hailed, surprisingly, from Catherine Walker. The contrasting white collars and bows did, however, detract from the bump, and the regulation flat pumps that had become her signature proved the perfect footwear for pregnancy.

**"YES PLEASE"** *(right)* So wrote Diana in her own hand on the original David Sassoon sketch for this maternity evening dress. "She was thrilled with it," he recalls. "She loved that particular wine-colored taffeta. When that dress was done, things were very romantic and buccaneerlike; we had a style in the ready-to-wear that was in that mood, and this was based on a particular dress in the collection that was featured in *Vogue*." This costume drama dress was worn to a charity evening at London's Barbican Centre in March 1982.

**PRETTY IN PINK** *(far right)* A favorite fuchsia-pink, nautical-style blousonned maternity dress by Catherine Walker, already seen at the wedding of flatmate Carolyn Pride, now appeared in its altered state for that regular Sunday pastime — spectator sporting at a polo match, when pregnant with Prince Harry.

bout of postnatal depression, which was hardly surprising, given the pressures in her newly married life to date. She barely had time to recoup her strength and adjust to motherhood before the start of the next hurdle—her first official overseas trip —a six-week tour of the Commonwealth, representing the Royal Family, scheduled for March 1983.

This will be a long haul, and the Princess has had precious little time

wise, at this stage, the Princess' taste has hardly progressed from dirndl skirts, plumed hats and predictable floaty evening frocks. From a fashion standpoint, the trip is fairly uneventful apart from one number.

This *pièce de resistance* was reserved for a dinner in Melbourne on the Wales' last night. On this occasion, Diana pulled out all the stops, appearing in a drop-dead-gorgeous long, white slinky one-

> ## "She was lovely, adored clothes, divine at a fitting; she seemed to enjoy it."
>
> GINA FRATINI

to evolve a style. She now needs a complete new wardrobe to take account of the contrasting elements Down Under—the heat of the Outback, the cooler climate in Alice Springs—notwithstanding the many round-the-clock official engagements for an entire six-week period.

At this point, the Princess widens her designer net to take in a clutch of new names—Victor Edelstein, Bruce Oldfield, Donald Campbell, Jasper Conran, Jan Vanvelden, Benny Ong, David Neill, Arabella Pollen, Gina Fratini, and Catherine Walker. And after much persuasion, little Prince William goes, too, although he will be based at Woomarga, a palatial homestead, with Nanny Barnes. Style-

sleeved, one-shouldered column dress, embroidered with silver and gold bugle beads. Designed by Hachi, this striking number exuded pure Hollywood glamor. It just oozed sensuality and was a style indicative of the Diana-to-be. That night, the royal screen-siren sent out the message, "I'll show you – I've got what it takes."

Her luggage also contained a pink and gold frilled, self-embossed long evening dress by Catherine Walker; a lipstick-pink organza long evening gown with shoestring straps and bow-tying shoulder straps by Edelstein that would reappear at La Scala, Milan, two years later—it was right at the time, but the sophisticated Milanese gave it the thumbs-down;

Catherine Walker's green and white polka-dot dress, with its contrasting white collar and tie, and worn with popsox to leave St. Mary's Hospital with her firstborn, was a decided mistake, compared with the stylish red crêpe coat by Jan Vanvelden that Diana sported the second-time around to cradle the newborn Harry.

The Princess' first public appearance post-William was at the Falkland Memorial Service at St.

Paul's, a month after the birth. Most moms take three months to get back into shape, and the Princess was no exception. She still had several pounds to shed, and the waist-emphasizing, cummerbund-style belt over a rather matronly bright blue dress was unflattering. Diana liked to accentuate her waistline, even though it was not one of her natural assets.

The Princess now had a healthy son and heir, but was suffering from a and a Bruce Oldfield dress of pale turquoise and silver Lurex with dinosaur frills that appeared at a charity ball in Sydney. Cinched with a wide silver leather belt, this showed that the Princess was still obsessed with waist emphasis.

More memorable still was Gina Fratini's long, cream satin dress with sheer, full organza sleeves and lace pintucked bodice. Diana wore it with the Queen Mary tiara and the Queen's Family Order, dazzling onlookers in Auckland.

This was the first dress Gina made for the Princess. "She was lovely, adored clothes, divine at a fitting; she seemed to enjoy it," says the designer. "She had a perfect figure, so there wasn't a problem. I adored her; she was so sweet, so friendly. There was never any question of feeling ill at ease, or nervous; she was always excited to see the clothes, chatted about them and her work; she had the most wonderful effect on people; you enjoyed meeting her and looked forward to the next time. If she hadn't seen you for a while, she would always have a little present; it was just great; she was lovely," she enthuses.

"After I shut down, I went on to do a collection for Hartnell, and the white dress that opened the Christie's auction—the sari-style, draped dress that I did for her—is the last time that I actually made a collection," remembers Gina. "I was delighted, because it was the first to go under the hammer and got the fourth highest bid. I was pleased because it had no association with anything in particular.

It wasn't a "Travolta," "Elvis," or "Divorce" dress. It was the original sample, and it fitted her beautifully. It was an incredibly hard dress to make, complicated with little criss crosses of draping. I offered to make her a new one, but she preferred to have the sample. It had only been worn on a model three times at the show. I always loved the first sample, there is something special about it, and I think we only had to do one tiny tweak.

"Diana was the perfect 10, my size 10 in every way, just the ideal person to dress; no designer could ask for more, and you couldn't be anything but nice about her; she was such a lovely girl; she had enthusiasm, a sense of fun; you couldn't help but love her; you always felt so special. She'd come bouncing in, greet you at the top of the stairs of KP," says Gina, with a lump in her throat. "Meeting her was something lovely that happened to my life."

Dutch designer Jan Vanvelden was another favorite at the time, and he was equally impressed. "A first, one

was a bit in awe of what she represented, but she always wanted to keep it low-key. We hit it off immediately, we really did. I was honored that she had chosen some of my clothes, particularly as I had just started out on my own; it was important for me to have such a famous client."

Jan received good press coverage

**A ROSY FUCHSIA** (above left) A girly, square-necked long pink organza evening dress, first seen in Brisbane in April 1983, was the first of many from the Victor Edelstein line.

**CRÈME DE LA CRÈME** (above) For a banquet in Auckland, the Princess wore Gina Fratini's regal cream satin dress with sheer organza sleeves and pretty pintuckery frosted with lace on the bodice, neckline, and cuffs.

**VANVELDEN'S FAVORITE** *(above)* A white and black cotton piqué, full-sleeved blouse in a print by Ascher—"I actually made that one again for the V&A Exhibition of Mr. Ascher," recalls Jan. This dramatic piece also went on the trip Down Under, as well as more casually to a polo match, worn with black leather, waist-whittling cummerbund and white pencil skirt.

**STAR TURN** *(left)* Of the entire Commonwealth wardrobe, this proved the glittering prize, the one and only Diana-design by the Japanese Hachi. It was to prove portentous, and was bought in Christie's auction for a reader competition by Britain's *Mail on Sunday*'s *You* magazine.

**WARM AND WONDERFUL** *(above)* Naive knit sheep sweater worn with a white blouse and black ribbon tie at neck and white jeans for watching polo at Smith's Lawn in June 1983.

**SPLENDOR ON THE GRASS** *(right)* In this endearing family snap of the Waleses and small son, William, in Auckland, Diana is wearing a her favorite Vanvelden, a full-sleeved, silk-spot dresses with white, pinked puritan collar.

from the photo call with Prince Charles and Prince William on the lawn of Government House in Auckland, when Princess Diana appeared in his green and white silk dress with contrasting serrated puritan collar. He also made her a yellow and white silk printed wing-collared dress that was seen in Alice Springs. "I made it into a blouse as well, and she wore that several times," he remembers.

Jan is convinced that the Waleses were in love at the beginning of the

marriage. "Whatever the world says, I truly believe that in the beginning they loved each other. I remember one time when I was doing fittings at the palace for one of the trips and Prince Charles burst in having just returned from Germany," he told me. "They were really surprised to see each other and genuinely hugged and kissed.

"The Princess was any designer's dream; there was nobody you would rather dress than the POW—obviously having known her has enriched my life. She was a very special person."

By the start of 1984, the Princess was pregnant again. Second time around, Diana knew the score, and there is a marked improvement in her wardrobe. She leaves the switch into loose-fitting styles as late as possible, until her fourth month.

A subtle, yet visible change is in her hair—the familiar bob was traded for a slightly longer, more feminine "groomed" look. Diana even acquired a taste for man's tailoring. When she was newly pregnant, a rock concert in Birmingham saw the first of several trend-setting tuxedo suits—Margaret Howell's white smoking jacket, paired with black tuxedo pants, a white shirt, and a black satin bow tie. A sharp, masculine/feminine modern look,

very Saint-Laurent inspired. Helped by Catherine Walker, Jan Vanvelden, and David Sassoon, plus her own experience, the Princess got it right this time around. Now more self-assured and adventurous, Diana

## "I truly believe that at the beginning they loved each other."

JAN VANVELDEN

adopted blouson styles that revealed her shape, rather than concealing her bulge under the flowing spotted tents favored in her first pregnancy.

The Waiting-for-Harry wardrobe really worked. Highlights were David

**INTRODUCING HARRY** (*left*) The red version — one of two easy smock-style crêpe coats worn over a striped dress with white collar and ribbon necktie by Vanvelden — was the choice for leaving St. Mary's Hospital and introducing Harry to the brave new world.

**BLOUSON STYLE** (*below left*) Catherine Walker's way with the bulge — if you've got if, flaunt it. A drop-waisted, ice-blue satin dress with blouson top, falling onto a pleated, hipline tying skirt.

**TUXEDO FUNCTION** (*far left*) The androgynous look was one that Diana espoused. This particular tuxedo pants suit, worn when pregnant with Harry, with an oversized white smoking jacket and black bow tie and pants, marked the first of many variations on the theme, and enabled the Princess to be modishly pregnant.

the Princess left St. Mary's Hospital with her second son, Harry. She had an heir and a spare, and this marked the happiest phase of her marriage.

Contrary to public opinion, Diana was not that extravagant with her clothes. "I would say that she was actually quite frugal, a hangover from her days of not having a lot to spend; no, perhaps somewhere between the two," comments David Sassoon.

Diana made an art form out of recycling. "She brought maternity dresses back to be altered; she didn't want to waste them. There was a Liberty print wool two-piece in silk jacquard, made for Trooping the Colour — a coral dress. I'd made the skirt shirred for her pregnancy, and later she said: 'Do you mind changing the skirt?' So we took the shirring out, and she wore it again," says Vanvelden.

Sassoon's romantic ivory chiffon Empire-line evening dress shot with metallic thread and set off with a tiara, worn to a dinner at the Royal Academy of Arts in London; Catherine Walker's ice-blue satin, wrap-style blousonned bodice dress, caught with a bow at the hipline, falling onto a pleated skirt, worn for the June premier of *Indiana Jones*; and fuchsia-pink, silk sailor dress with detachable white collar, also blouson style; and Vanvelden's coral pink suit with a loose, tunic top, falling onto a softly pleated skirt.

Jan's easy, fine wool crêpe coats with pintucked, smock-style shoulder line were favorites that served the Princess well through this second pregnancy. She had the same style in navy and in pillarbox red. The first was worn for a visit to Warrington over a white wing-collared cotton shirt. The classical navy and white theme was echoed by a Freddie Fox veiled, bicolored tilted hat. The red version, worn over a red and white striped dickey dress, appeared when

"THE PRINCESS WAS VERY EASY; we got on with each other straight away and we lasted a long time—10 or 11 years. The first visible outfit of mine was made in 1981. I made her a navy-blue, silk-velvet suit with culottes and a little boxy jacket," remembers Oldfield. "She wore it to turn on the Christmas lights in London's Regent Street."

Of the 50 or 60 outfits he made for her, Bruce singles out "the one-shoulder dress that she wore to Guildhall in November 1982, when everyone was alerted to her anorexia," as his most memorable early design. "She did fluctuate in weight so much. Basically, she was big-boned and had a big frame. I always put her at 26 to 27-inch waist, a nice meaty 10-12, and I am fairly generous in my sizing—she was long in the arm and had long legs from waist to thigh, though

# Bruce OLDFIELD

**THE FAIRY-TALE PRINCESS** (above) In a long turquoise and silver flecked evening dress with dinosaur frills, with silver leather cummerbund.

she did have this tendency to lock her legs backward on parade, which caused straight skirts to look bad, as she stuck her legs out and her hips forward. She also inclined toward "hunching," something I was constantly berating her for. But she could take a joke and I told her, 'you'll thank me when you're 35.'

"Of my designs, my particular favorite was for the first Birthright Ball at the Albert Hall in the mid to late eighties – it was a long, red crêpe dress, ruched up the front with big shoulders, a slash down the front and a big slit at the back," he recalls. "She quite liked bright colors; I wasn't averse to her wearing red; I never particularly saw her in pastels, more bright, sharp shades.

"The Princess must have liked the purple ruched velvet, off-the-shoulder dress (Lot No. 73 in the auction), because it came out a few times."

The erstwhile Barnardo Boy reckons that dressing the Princess probably did change the direction of his life. "It is that double-edged sword —one didn't want to be thought of as just making royal dresses for a single client. You didn't want that tag, but, on the other hand, it didn't do you any harm, not in terms of column inches and celebrity abroad," he concedes.

"The POW was a one-woman-star show. She has left a huge void. There just isn't that one person that everyone can focus on to see what is happening in "dressy" frocks," he believes. "I don't think that I was ever responsible

**DYNASTY DI** (above) This red silk dress with defined shoulder line, draped bodice detail, deep V back and center front slit, is one of the designer's personal favorites.

for putting her in anything "frilly"— rather the reverse. I was always trying to make her look sexy, never romantic; the English rose syndrome was never my bag. I liked to see her in much simpler things. When I was dressing her she couldn't wear clothes as décolleté as she did in the latter years. After all, at the time, she was the future Queen of England," he says.

On reflection, says Oldfield: "I think that we were a constant throughout the eighties; even though the Princess may have changed allegiance. It is a shame that I was thrown out

**BLUE ALERT** *(above)* The dress that sparked off fears of Diana's anorexia—electric blue, circle-print crêpe-de-chine long evening dress with a one-shoulder Lei-style ruffled bodice, and skirt with asymmetrical hemline, worn in 1982.

**SWEETPAPER PRINCESS** *(left)* Diana gets Bruce Oldfield's Midas touch with a metallic lamé, Fortuny-pleated, long evening dress with V-neckline and Odeon-style draping detail. This made its début at a Dr. Barnardo's Ball at London's Grosvenor House Hotel in March 1985.

with the bathwater, but that's the way it crumbles," he says stoically. "But we did run through that whole period. We were on a journey, and Diana was on a journey to find her sense of style. She was pretty up and down in the way that she presented herself in the middle years, and she did make some horrible mistakes, anomalies that went on throughout the 1980s. With Catherine Walker, she found her style, but we were all on that journey."

# chapter three
## déjà vu ...

"You're going to see everything time and time again, because it fits, it's comfortable, and it still works."

DIANA, PRINCESS OF WALES

# Recycling a Royal Wardrobe

**PUT YOUR MONEY ON A WINNER** *(above)* Take one dalmatian-spot dress by Victor Edelstein and get three-years' life out of it—that's fashion mileage for you, and a husband's delight. Worn here with a ruffled, peplum-effect overskirt for a flutter at The Derby in June 1986, this was an outfit that would be seen again—and again.

**ENCORE** *(previous page)* That same polka dot dress (spot-on, again), this time hatless in a more throwaway way, at Windsor Polo a year later (1987). The apron-style skirt has been replaced by Diana's favorite signature cummerbund effect waist, achieved by draping treatment.

MOTHERHOOD LENT the Princess of Wales a new dimension. Diana became preoccupied with Princes William and Harry, "Her Boys," and less concerned with the state of her own personal wardrobe. She did, however, take to heart the harsh public criticism of her so-called lavish fashion expenditure. Constantly in the public eye, the Princess was in an invidious position. Whatever she did, the poor girl really couldn't win. A posse of new fashions and she would be branded a spendthrift; a dearth of new clothes with which to stun the public and the Princess wasn't living up to her magical fairy-tale image.

Diana deemed it politically correct to take a leaf out her mother-in-law the Queen's book, and she made a deliberate effort to embark on a new stringent frugality. Clothes were constantly recycled, and 'The More You See It' became her fashion maxim, as she veered steadily toward the maternal image, eschewing that of the "material girl."

"Well, I'm afraid that you're going to see everything time and time again, because it fits, it's comfortable, and it still works," Diana promised. "You know I feel that a lot of people thought that I was going on a fashion tour for two weeks. I wasn't. I was going along to support the British flag, with my husband, as his wife. My clothes were far from my mind," said Princess Diana, in an attempt to put the record straight following her Italian trip in April 1985.

She had come under heavy fire from the press for spending a mythical $128,000 on her new wardrobe for the official tour.

The Princess sets out to redress the balance, and prove that she is not merely a glamorous clotheshorse and international cover-girl, but rather the world's most famous working mother and wife. As she grows in stature and matures into this new role, the Princess starts to reinvent her wardrobe.

Recycling, or putting a new spin on a tried-and-tested outfit, is something the Princess would continue to do throughout her 16-year long career.

Diana began to revive a number of her favorite existing outfits. Many were given a new lease of life; others were passed on to sisters, Sarah and Jane, or to her closest friends. "Play it again, Diana" became her new game in an attempt to avoid censure.

Outfits would be transformed subtly—a different collar, another jacket, the addition or subtraction of a peplum, as with Victor Edelstein's much-flaunted polka-dot dress. On other occasions, the Princess would make the changes simply by wearing an outfit in a new way or with different accessories—a tiara, an alternative hat, jewelery, or hairstyle.

Those outfits that enjoyed the most public encores simply came out again for yet more accolades.

"She did recycle her clothes," confirms David Sassoon. "That same christening outfit was recycled in Sydney in March 1983, as was the long red and gold spotted dress.

"The funny thing is that she did not make heavy weather of clothes; she didn't seem to take fashion all that seriously, though she thought it was quite fun. Other members of the Royal Family would make such a fuss, whereas the Princess would come in at

## "She didn't seem to take fashion all that seriously."

DAVID SASSOON

the last minute with 'I have such and such an occasion to go to and I need something. I had completely forgotten,' " observes Sassoon.

David Sassoon's own pieces were recurrent in the Princess' working wardrobe, such as her official engagement outfit—the navy crêpe sailor suit that was to reappear a month later on a visit to Cheltenham. The cantaloupe-melon colored "going-away" outfit, cannily ordered with two jackets of varying sleeve lengths, was another example of Diana's recycling. The short-sleeved

**ONCE MORE, WITH FEELING** First seen at Prince William's christening, in 1982 *(above)*, David Sassoon's lipstick-pink, sprig-print battle-dress jacket and camisole dress was worn again at the Sydney Opera House in March 1983 *(top)*, set off with John Boyd's wide-brimmed hat and worn with white clutch bag and low-heeled pumps.

**SPOT THE DIFFERENCE** *(left)* This time minus the peplum, the draped cummerbund effect lends the dress Diana's favorite waist emphasis—a winner for Royal Ascot in June 1988.

jacket went on the honeymoon in July 1981; the long-sleeved version would reemerge two years later, worn on the Australian tour.

Originally made as part of her wedding trousseau, the "Gonzaga" evening dress, as it became known, was another Sassoon favorite,

the following year–this time worn with different jewelery. It was revived yet again in November 1984 for Diana's appearance at the Royal Command Performance.

The most irrepressible dress was, according to Sassoon, "one that she wore over and over for a period of

## "She had a practical streak ... a lot of common sense."

DAVID SASSOON

appearing over and over again. It made its debut at the Victoria and Albert Museum in November 1981. On this occasion it was worn with a gemstoned, multistrand pearl choker. The dress turned up again at the film premier of *Gandhi* in December of

**THE ONE THAT WENT AWAY** The short-sleeved version of Diana's cantaloupe-melon colored "going away" suit *(above)* with white ruffle trim by David Sassoon was worn again in July 1983 *(right)*. The long-sleeved style had to wait until the royal tour that took the Princess to Australia in 1983.

**SECOND SIGHTING** *(left)* That Gonzaga saga went to the premier of the film *Gandhi* in December 1982. Sassoon's vision of a fairy-tale princess in pretty pastelry of pale blue and pink and white chiffon found expression in a long evening dress with off-the-shoulder neckline, the waist caught with a blue satin sash, falling onto a full skirt with a ruffled hemline and subtle silver beading.

**STILL GOING STRONG** *(above)* And the same dress appeared at the Royal Command Performance in 1984, after the Princess had grown out her familiar girly bob hairstyle into a longer, more sophisticated style.

**"VERY ENDEARING, VERY ENDURING"**

So ran the *Daily Mail* headline above an article
quipping "Yes, it's That Dress again." This royal
blue, short-sleeved crêpe-de-chine dress went to
church in Sydney, Australia, in January 1988 *(top)*;
to polo at Smith's Lawn in June of the same year
*(above)*; and on a visit to AIDS patients in São
Paolo, Brazil, in April 1991 *(right)*.

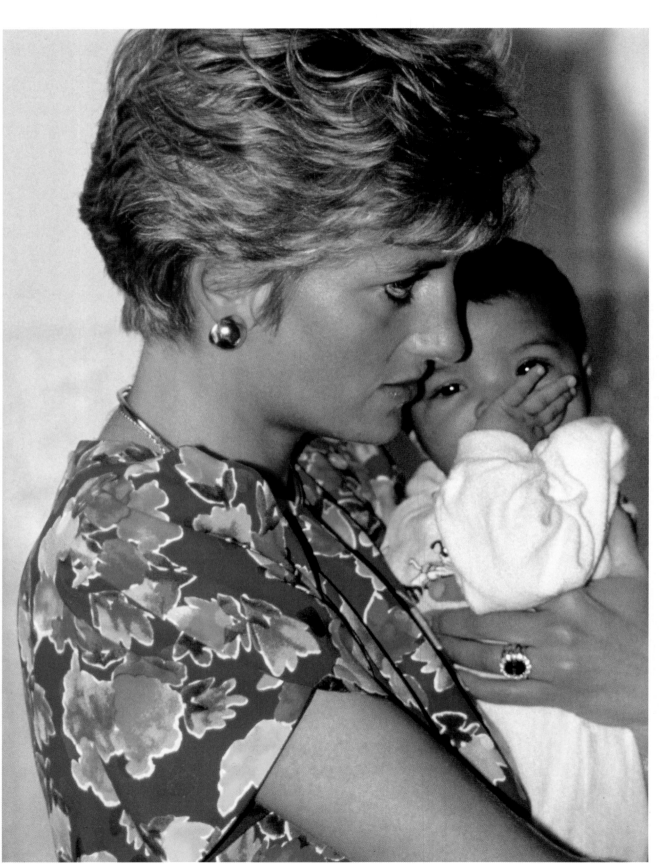

five years, 1988-1992, to so-called 'caring' occasions." In royal blue crêpe-de-chine, and printed with multibright flowers, it featured short sleeves and a ruched waistline. This was a dress the Princess particularly liked, as she considered it neither too outrageous, nor too intrusive.

*Match* for $42,000. The magazine held a competition, and the winner re-sold the dress. "I didn't mind; I was very happy if it did some good; I think that the whole idea was excellent," comments Lorcan. Sassoon's last dress for the Princess also went to the auction—a long, draped black slip-

## "I was trying to do a tuxedo, but make it feminine."

LORCAN MULLANY

The dress made its debut in January 1988. It reappeared at a polo match in June of that same year. In 1990 it showed up on visits to a London shelter for homeless, and a London neighborhood. It flew to Brazil in 1991, and also put in an appearance at a charity event in July 1992.

The first outfit designed by Sassoon's partner, Lorcan Mullany for the Princess was a huge success—a dress that resembled a two-piece with black lace-sequin bodice and white satin, black bow-trimmed collar and cuffs, with a short black satin pencil skirt. "I was trying to do a tuxedo, but make it feminine, so we had the idea of putting it off the shoulder," explains the designer.

"She wore it a lot," he concedes. "I think that the Princess saw it in *Harper's* and rang up for it; it was off-the-peg, and there must be a lot of them about," he recalls. Described in the Christie's auction catalogue as "a short, formal cocktail dress in black and white," it was bought by *Paris*

dress with be-jeweled shoulder straps. This was first worn to the Coliseum, in London, in 1987, reappeared in 1991 on an official visit to Canada, and went to *Romeo and Juliet* in June 1993.

Polka dots were always a winner at the races. The Edelstein dress was sported at the Derby in June 1986, with a peplum overskirt effect and flying-saucer style hat. It also ran at a Windsor polo match a year later. This

**MAGIC IN BLACK & WHITE** Lorcan Mullany's popular dress was first seen at the London City Ballet in October 1989 *(above)*. It reappeared a year later at Sadler's Wells, and then at a charity evening for the British Lung Foundation in October 1990 *(left)*. It enjoyed a *Children of Eden* showing in January of the following year, and then accompanied Diana and Prince Harry to a concert at Wembley in October 1991 *(far left)*. Like many of the Princess' favorite evening dresses, it went under the hammer (as Lot No. 4) at Christie's auction in 1997.

**BACK TO THE FUCHSIA** *(above)* Victor
Edelstein's familiar pintucked, fuchsia-pink dress,
first sighted in Australia, also went to a Barry
Manilow concert. It turned up again here, for a
night at the opera—La Scala, Milan—in 1985, lent
the full treatment with The Queen Mary Tiara
(Diana's present from The Queen in 1981) and
drop diamond and pearl earrings, with a pearl
choker. The dress was deemed disappointing by
the Milanese *fashionista*.

**SASSOON'S SLIP-DRESS** *(right)* This would be
the final dress that Bellville-Sassoon/Lorcan Mullany
would design for the Princess—"a cherubic black
and gold evening dress" is its description as Lot
No. 77 in the Christie's auction catalogue, where it
ended up selling for $23,000. Made for Diana in
October 1987, for the English National Ballet's
*Romeo and Juliet* at The Coliseum, the same dress
also went on an official visit to Canada in 1991.

**TUX DE LUX** *(above)* Victor Edelstein's witty variation on the tuxedo theme made its debut, appropriately, at the premier of *Dangerous Liaisons* (which was the object of the design exercise) in 1989, worn with an upswept coiffure, and black satin opera gloves. It reappeared, more informally, in 1991 at the premier of *Rambling Rose*, worn with a new cropped hairdo and bare arms. It raised $31,050 in the Christie's auction.

time a design alteration gave the dress a cummerbunded waist treatment, and it was set off by loose hair and a single rope of pearls. It was to make a reappearance at the Royal Ascot races the following year.

Edelstein designed some of the most memorable dresses for the Princess—his variation on a tailcoat theme—a long, black strapless velvet dress with contrast facing and three paste buttons shone at the premier of *Dangerous Liaisons* in 1989 and also went to the first night of *Rambling Rose* in 1991. His oyster-colored Duchesse satin long, formal dinner-dress with matching bolero, exquisitely embroidered by Hurel, graced the state banquet hosted by President and Madame Mitterand at the Elysée Palace in 1988, and was worn again at the Wintergarden in New York City.

One of Victor's early dresses—a square-necked, fuchsia pink organza long evening gown with shoulder bow ties—was first seen in Brisbane, Australia, in 1983. It made a comeback at La Scala, in Milan, in 1985.

It was double-duty, too, for Jacques Azagury's blue-on-black, velvet-bodiced galactic dance-dress, falling onto a two-tiered ballet-style skirt of electric-blue organza. It first appeared in Florence in 1985, then Toronto a year later. The glittering prize—a show-stopping, slinky, beaded white one-shouldered, one-sleeved columnar dinner-dress by Hachi made its debut in Australia in 1983. The same year, it attended the premier of *Octopussy*. It shimmered its way through a dinner at the National Gallery in Washington D.C.

**LOOKS FAMILIAR?** *(top and above)* Well, it is, but circumstances change. This Vanvelden wool crêpe dress, originally worn for Diana's second pregnancy, in 1984, reappeared as a sailor dress in Mildura, Australia, in November 1985. She also made changes with her headwear, recycling the John Boyd hat with and without its dotty veil.

IN THE PINK Catherine Walker's rose pink/white striped suit with full, dirndl style skirt, cropped jacket, puff sleeves was first worn on the 1983 Australian tour *(left)*, accompanied by a pink skull cap by John Boyd, with white pumps and bag. It is seen here *(far left)* in an altered state two years later, with a pleated skirt and sou'wester with plumed, turnback brim by John Boyd, worn to visit an orange grove in Catania, Sicily, in 1985.

Breton hat with contrast maroon trim, making it appear more streamlined. Dutch-born designer Jan Vanvelden's hyacinth-blue crêpe maternity two-piece was made with a white puritan collar and jacket in 1984; a year later it was totally transformed into a sailor dress, the jacket discarded, and the collar replaced.

For the official Australian trip in 1983, a pink Catherine Walker dress softly belted and full-skirted, was straw cartwheel hat. The loose, easy style made it an easy convert for maternity wear—it went to a Duran Duran concert in July 1983, and reappeared as a maternity dress for polo at Windsor in 1984 when the Princess was pregnant with Harry.

Catherine Walker was, without doubt, the all-out royal designer favorite. She must take credit for some of the most opulent, and yet simple, gowns worn by the Princess.

## "She gave an enormous boost to the millinery industry."

GRAHAM SMITH, MILLINER

in 1985, and returned to Australia that same year. The dress was to enjoy yet another outing in July 1996.

Caroline Charles' pale camel, belted bathrobe coat first appeared in 1981, set off with white cockade-trimmed hat by John Boyd; the same coat made a comeback four years later, this time worn with an upturned

worn, accessorized with a small, perched white and pink hat. Two years later, the same dress went to Italy—this time sporting a tightly-pleated skirt set off with a wide-brimmed, pink straw sou'wester hat.

Walker's shocking-pink crêpe-de-chine sailor dress with detachable white collar and blousonned-style, elasticated drop-waistline and pleated skirt, was first seen at the wedding of the Princess' flatmate, Carolyn Pride, in 1982, worn with a white and black

Most of these were recycled. The celebrated 'Elvis' dress—a strapless white shimmery sheath with cropped, bolero-style jacket—made its debut at the British Fashion Awards at the Royal Albert Hall in 1989. It then went on to Hong Kong and later attended several film premiers. The designer's ice-blue draped silk-chiffon long evening dress, redolent of Hollywood heroine, Grace Kelly, went to the Cannes Film Festival in 1987, and to the premier of *Miss*

**JEWEL ON THE TOWN ... THE ELVIS DRESS**

*(right and below)* This glittering prize was actually commissioned for the Princess' official tour to Hong Kong, but Diana obviously couldn't wait to wear it and jumped the gun. The "Elvis" dress, as it came to be nicknamed by the fashion press, made its debut at the British Fashion Awards, at the Royal Albert Hall in October 1989. One of Catherine Walker's most spectacular creations, it was one of the hits of the Christie's auction, where it sold for a cool $151,000, a close second to the "Travolta" dress.

**VIVA ESPAÑA** *(left)* Stendhal-esque shades of "Le Rouge et Le Noir" for Murray Arbeid's black velvet bodiced Lady-of-Spain-style dress with layered net skirts and rise 'n fall hemline. This bicolored flamenco ballgown went to the America's Cup Ball in September 1986. It caused a sensation worn with deliberately mismatched statement satin gloves, one red, the other black; a black ribbon choker, centered with paste brooch; drop earrings from her paste collection; and upswept hair. The same dramatic dress added *couleur locale* in Spain the following year, and was to fetch $25,300 at the Christie's auction

**TWINKLE, TWINKLE, LITTLE STAR** *(far left and below left)* This kingfisher sequin-scaled mermaiden dress with décolleté neckline and center-front slit was first sighted in Vienna in 1986, when Diana's hair was longer and more "coiffed." It came out for an encore at a film premier in December 1990, and again in 1993. Yet another design from the prolific Catherine Walker, it fetched $24,150 in the Christie's auction.

*Saigon* in 1989. Walker's kingfisher sequinned and ruched mermaid number saw the premier of *Biggles* in May 1986; it went to Vienna that same year, and to the Diamond Ball in 1990. Murray Arbeid's dramatic flamenco-inspired balldress also turned up at a film premier in September 1986, and went on an official visit to Spain a year later.

Many of these dresses went under the hammer at Christie's auction in 1997. They have all done their bit for charity; some are still doing it. If only they could talk, they would have some incredible stories to tell. Now they, too, have been recycled and belong to another time, another place.

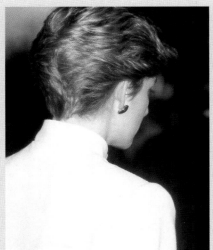

# Making
# HEADLINES

From girlhood locks to short, sharp chic, Diana's changing hairstyles (from left to right) …

**TWEENAGE TRESSES** Lady Diana Spencer had an inherent sense of style—her straight hair is shoulder-length, with a long, side-swept fringe.

**SLOANEY BOB** March 1981, and that much-cloned Kevin Shanley cut—the young, wash 'n' wear hair with layered bangs, from the New Romantic, pre-wedding, 'Shy Di' days.

**FORTIES STYLE** When Prince Harry was born, Diana fancied a change of hair—the longest she would ever wear it during her royal years.

**SHORT WAVELENGTH** And at the end of the 1986 summer recess at Balmoral, the Princess sported her shortest style to date, cropped all round and cut like a duck's tail at the neck.

IF WE COULDN'T afford the designer dresses, we could at least aspire to those trademark tresses. Diana's wardrobe may have been largely aspirational, but her hairstyles were inspirational, creating an immediate demand for look-alike styles.

As a child, Lady Diana Spencer had worn her hair long, but from her early teenage years, she sported that easy, wash 'n' wear hair, a signature Sloaney bob, with chunky sunstreaks and heavy bangs that served as a security blanket from a prying world.

At the time of her engagement, Lady Diana Spencer frequented the South Kensington salon of Headlines where crimper Kevin Shanley styled her barnet fair. He did the honors for the wedding and became the

Princess' personal coiffeur, and he accompanied Diana on numerous official engagements and tours in the early years of her marriage.

Shortly after the wedding, the Princess grew her layers a little longer and started wearing her hair in a softer, fluffier, more feminine style, with more sophisticated, less defined, side-swept bangs. It became distinctly blonder and she continued to wear a variation of this look throughout both her pregnancies.

Women always seem to crave a change of hair after they've given birth, and, soon after Harry's arrival, the Princess let hers grow to its longest yet. Shanley swept the familiar fringe to one side, and curled the shoulder-length tresses softly, flicking

them behind the ears, secured with combs on each side of the parting.

The result was a style redolent of that worn by Forces sweethearts in the forties. Though feminine and dramatically different for Diana, it did not meet with public approval. The people wanted the Princess they knew and loved, so the Populist Princess reverted to form with a variation on her signature style.

Due to his family commitments, Kevin Shanley was replaced in late 1984 by Richard Dalton, a fellow stylist at the same salon, who was to have Diana's head in his capable hands for almost a decade. Dalton made his presence felt with toned-down color, a more swept-back style, and a soft, volume-adding perm.

The next memorable headliner was Di's D.A. (Duck's A***), inspired by the "teddy-boy" style of the fifties. Her hair was cropped all over, particularly around the ears, and dovetailed into a tail effect at the nape of the neck. It was designed to prove very practical for the upcoming trip to the Gulf States, but it needed careful blow-drying to achieve the desired effect.

Diana's hair had to look good "au naturel," under both hats and tiaras, and in 1986, blonde highlights complemented a style featuring shorter, backswept layers at front and sides, with more length at the back.

The Princess looked stunning with wet hair, albeit by default. A classic example took place when she was drenched en route to Luciano Pavarotti's open air concert in London's Hyde Park in 1991; she looked dynamite, very fresh and natural in her navy velvet tuxedo pants-suit, despite the dousing.

Being more relaxed about her hair was something that the Princess learned from supermodels super-stylist, Sam McKnight. They met on a *Vogue* cover-shoot in 1990, for that memorable bare-shouldered, tiara'd Patrick Demarchelier picture that

confirmed that she was indeed both supermodel and covergirl material.

"Hello, I'm Diana. What can you do with my mop?" she asked Sam quizzically. For the cover-shoot, McKnight styled Di's hair in a far more natural way, despite the tiara. She must have been duly impressed,

## "I told her that it was the way to wow them."

### SAM MCKNIGHT

for at the end of the shoot, the Princess gave him "carte blanche" to restyle her crowning glory, marking the start of a relationship that would last for the rest of her life.

Sam gave the Princess' hair the chop and revolutionized the way she wore it, and told her that she had a great head of hair, liberating her from all that titivating and lacquering.

This new-found, free-wheeling hairstyle coincided with the new independent Diana. In 1990, she wore her hair boyishly cropped, helmet-like straight and fringed; in 1991 she sported a style that was even shorter, multilayered, and spiky.

"After she and Charles separated in 1992, we lightened the color and grew it a bit longer so that it looked more feminine," admitted Sam.

"After her divorce, she went to New York and I persuaded her to appear with her hair slicked right back," he says.

That was for the Gala Ceremony of the Council of the Fashion Designers of America, at New York's Lincoln Center, when Diana honored her good friend Liz Tilberis, editor of American *Harper's Bazaar*, with a special award.

For the occasion, the Princess wore her hair slicked-back with gel, "au naturel," and she looked like a million dollars, the new dynamic Diana, a global figure, confident and contemporary.

Those sun-streaked tresses were, without doubt, her crowning glory—she looked better with casual, free-flowing windswept hair than with all

**THAI DI ...** The Princess who dined in Bangkok looked every inch the part. Colored silk flowers lent an exotic twist and a touch of *couleur locale* to a hairstyle caught at one side.

**SLICKED BACK CHIC** "I'd often done it for her in private, and kept telling her she looked gorgeous, but until then, she hadn't had the courage to go out with it like that," recalls Sam McKnight of the CFDA Awards in New York.

**JUST ADD WATER** The wet look may have been highly fashionable, but in this instance it was more by accident than design. The heavens opened and Diana got a drenching as she arrived at Pavarotti's open air concert in London's Hyde Park. And she still looked divine, "au naturel."

**BEYOND THE FRINGE** For a trip to preview Christie's New York auction, the fringe was back again, a neat chin-level bob held in place with a modish hairband —a blonde version of US *Vogue* editor Anna Wintour's signature style.

the titfers and tiaras. It was all a matter of downsizing. Just as she shrugged off her past with the sale of her evening gowns in the cathartic Christie's auction, so it was with her hair—simple, more manageable do-it-yourself styles began to eclipse the more studied styles.

# chapter four
# daring di ...

"Sometimes I can be a little outrageous,
which is quite nice. Sometimes."

DIANA, PRINCESS OF WALES

# Dynamite Di

**DRESSING UP IS DRESSING GOWN** *(above)*
"I didn't have the nerve to wear the trousers," the
Princess confessed to designer David Sassoon,
so the fuchsia/cobalt/turquoise checked Madras
silk dressing-gown went on the town solo and
"sans pantalon" for a Fashion Week reception at
Lancaster House in March 1988. The dress has
quilted shawl collar and cuffs, and a traditional
tasseled tie-belt.

**"SHE HAS AN ELECTRIC SMILE"** So said
celebrated photographer Patrick Demarchelier of
his subject *(previous page)*. This magical shot of
the Princess appeared in the December 1990
issue of glossy *Vogue*, when Liz Tilberis was
editor. This happy, relaxed picture, marked a new
informality, albeit with a tiara. Had Tilberis had her
way, it would have made the Christmas 1990
cover but, sadly, the Queen vetoed it.

"I CAN'T ALWAYS WEAR what I'd like to
an engagement, because it's just not
practical. There is only one golden
rule—clothes are for the job. They've
got to be practical," stressed the
Princess. However, Diana did admit,
with a twinkle in her eye: "Sometimes
I can be a little outrageous, which is
quite nice. Sometimes."

Royal dressing was a matter of
"clotheshorses for courses," as the
event or occasion determined the
dress code, but the Princess did,
nevertheless, allow herself to indulge
in certain high-fashion looks and to
customize them.

Diana assumed the role of royal
style-setter, one that afforded her
more freedom of self-expression than
any other young royal to date. It
worked, and proved advantageous for
Britain's global image.

The House of Windsor needed
modernizing; the royals were ripe for
a face-lift and Diana would be their
lodestar. The Princess was allowed, to
a great degree, to be a free spirit, at
least fashionwise.

The girl couldn't help looking the
part; try as she may to play down
her stylishness, be low-key, and
project herself as a workhorse, she
was, despite all the protestations, a
natural clotheshorse.

Though the Princess could not
allow herself to be totally provocative,
really risqué, or outrageously outré in
her dress, there were times when she
bent the rules and sailed pretty close
to the wind.

For example, the Princess of Wales is
invited to be guest of honor at a
reception at Lancaster House to
celebrate London Fashion Week in
March 1988. This will be attended by
the leading lights in the British
fashion industry, a clutch of top
designers, British and foreign press.

Given the occasion, how should
Diana dress? This was the perfect
opportunity for Diana to lend free
rein to her own personal taste and
style, and come up with an individual
fashion statement.

With the fashion groupies out in
force, whatever Diana wore would be
heavily scrutinized and criticized,

York designer, Ralph Lauren, was
advocating this particular look.

Although not totally convinced,
the Princess, nevertheless, went along
with the idea. Based on an Edwardian
gentleman's housecoat, the result was
a dressing-gown dress, with contrast
quilted shawl collar, cinched with
tasseled cord, to be worn over
matching slacks.

Well, that was the idea, but,
"I didn't have the nerve to wear the
slacks," the Princess confessed to
David at Lancaster House.

In the penultimate years of her
short life, Diana acquired nerve and
verve, and being Di-rectional became

> "In the nicest possible way, she
> is well aware that she is a dish."
>
> CLIVE JAMES

written about and photographed. She
was in something of a dilemma due to
this pressure, so she sought advice
from her tried-and-trusted designer
David Sassoon. Over a discussion at
his studio, a particular fabric caught
the Princess' eye.

"I love the material—what can we
do with it?" the Princess asked
quizzically, referring to a woven
checked satin fabric composed of
vivid blues and fuchsias.

"The dressing-gown look, worn
over trousers, is very fashionable,"
suggested Sassoon. At the time, New

second nature to her. According to
comedienne and erstwhile school-
friend Harriet Bowden, Diana was
"into breaking the rules," but
essentially, she was pretty much
establishment. Nonetheless, there
were indeed occasions when she
would spring surprises on the
fashion world.

Sometimes they worked, and
sometimes they didn't. For Diana,
being directional meant giving a nod
in the direction of high fashion, going
out on a limb for a look, or endorsing
a trend of the moment.

**PUFFBALL PRINCESS** Catherine Walker's nautical-striped puffball dress with coordinating, long-line, brass-buttoning naval blazer was worn on a trip to Portugal in February 1987 *(top)*. The same dress *(above)* was worn with a cream blazer to the Cannes Film Festival in May 1987.

**INSPIRED BY THE BALLETS RUSSES** *(right)* The Emanuels' corset-topped ballgown first appeared at a Red Cross Ball in July 1986; it also went to a Bond premier in June 1987.

**CORSET-STYLE COCKTAIL SHAKER** (right)
The inspirations for Catherine Walker's corset-bodiced, slip-skirted dress in bitextured velvet and lace were clearly borrowed from the boudoir. The corset-top's scalloped neckline is echoed on the hemline of the skirt.

That Sassoon dressing-gown dress was one such design. Another memorable example was Catherine Walker's striped puffball or "pouffe"-skirted dress, in bold navy and white stripes, worn with a nautical brass-buttoning blazer. This outfit first showed up at Toulouse, and then again in Portugal in February 1987.

The lingerie look was another directional trend that Diana espoused. A "corset-top" cropped up in white from the Emanuels' Diaghilev Collection in the form of a white and gold embroidered bodice on a dress worn to a London event in 1986.

For an AIDS gala, in 1991, the Princess appeared in a Catherine Walker wine-colored dress with scalloped corset-top, falling onto a short, slip-style skirt of tonal lace, the scalloping repeated on the hemline. The contrast of heavy and light worked brilliantly. The style proved innovatory, yet modish—the perfect balance for the Princess.

The long, midnight-blue, lace-frosted silk slip-dress, created by John Galliano, that the Princess wore on the occasion of the New York Fashion Awards in December 1996, was an outfit that caused a lot of controversy.

**OVER OR UNDER?** *(left)* Fashion's erstwhile foundations were making news as outerwear. Diana was privileged in that this long Dior navy slip-dress, designed by John Galliano (far left), was to be the first outfit to hail from the House's Couture atelier. Rumor has it that it was *Harper's Bazaar* editor, Liz Tilberis, pictured center left, who cajoled Diana into wearing Galliano to the New York Fashion Awards, held at the Metropolitan Museum of Modern Art.

Newly appointed to the House of Dior, John Galliano was a tour de force, the most directional designer of the day, so it seemed only fitting that Diana be seen to acknowledge this great British talent by wearing one of his creations.

While it seemed like a great idea at the time, with hindsight, it was decidedly a fashion faux-pas. "It" girls can get away with a creation like this, but not princesses.

Rumor has it that this slip-dress was worn at the prompting of Diana's good friend, Liz Tilberis, editor of *Harper's Bazaar*. On the grapevine, the word was out that Diana proposed wearing this particular style, and designer Roberto Devorik tried unsuccessfully to persuade other designers to talk her out of it.

According to Tomasz Starzewski: "Liz Tilberis was very manipulative—I believe it was she who cajoled the Princess into wearing Galliano, that slip-dress from Dior; there was an inner bodice, but she never wore it."

And in consequence, the Galliano dress looked baggy and ill-fitting on the Princess' bustline.

**SO SAD** *(right)* The perennial Chanel "sad-occasion" belted wool crêpe coat dress, with black satin shawl-collared, long-line, double-breasted jacket, was worn with a striking, black straw, wide-brimmed hat to the funeral of Japan's Emperor Hirohito in November 1990.

**GOYA DRESS** *(far right)* The Princess looks ace in wicked black lace—a front-on-view of Victor Edelstein's long dress, inspired by those worn by Goya's Spanish dancers. The shoulder-revealing bodice falls onto a flounced, lace skirt, and the lace is layered over magenta silk, lending the illusion of bronze.

Directional though the dress may have been, the style was just not flattering to Diana's silhouette. Slip-dresses are far more suited to a waif-like woman of the Kate Moss mold than to a broad-shouldered, well worked-out lady like Diana.

Dynamite, or statement, dressing was the Princess' fashion strong point, and her short life was punc-

> ## "She did try to wear the right thing for the right occasion."
>
> GRAHAM SMITH

tuated by several dramatic, show-stopping numbers.

Dresses such as dreams are made of, these were usually drop-dead gorgeous entrance-makers, and they often appeared at the great milestones in Diana's life.

The controversial "Engagement" dress, by the Emanuels, with its dramatically daring décolletage,

marked the first of this ilk; this was followed by the "Woman in White"—the long, ice-frosted Hachi column dress that made the first of its many stunning appearances in Sydney. Catherine Walker's white "Elvis" dress was another shining example; so too was Christina Stambolian's "wicked" little black, body-wrapping number that came to

be dubbed the "Divorce" dress. Like most beautiful young women, Diana always looked magic in black, be it at an official function or a funeral.

Oldfield's long, glamorous, gold Fortuny pleated dress; Edelstein's velvet "Travolta" number, and his black lace "Goya-esque" dress are just three more examples of the style that sums up "Dynamite Di."

At home, or abroad, Diplomatic Di was yet another aspect of the Princess' evolving style.

Suitability was her strong point, and she would use fashion as the medium to communicate her message.

Her wardrobe, usually conceived in conjunction with Catherine Walker, was always cleverly worked out so her clothes paid tribute to the country that she was visiting, as a mark of respect from guest to host. It always appeared as though the Princess had made a special effort, which indeed she had. Call it environmental dressing, if you like. This was a role the Princess played to perfection, and had done right from the very start.

A flashback to her first official visit to Wales, in 1981, is a classic example—Diana incorporated the Welsh national colors into her Donald Campbell red and green suit, with a red fitted jacket, paired with a bottle green pleated skirt.

For a visit to a naval base at La Spezia, Italy, in April 1985, a cream and navy striped Catherine Walker coat-dress, set-off with a cheeky "doughboy" hat, a cute upturned bob cap by British milliner Graham Smith, was salutary.

The calf-length black lace dress and mantilla-style veil by Catherine Walker Diana wore for an audience with the Pope at the Vatican on the same trip, could not have proved more appropriate. It was a case of when in Rome ...

**PAPAL PROTOCOL** *(above)* To visit the Pope at The Vatican in April 1985, the Princess dressed appropriately. For this special meeting, Catherine Walker designed a politically correct, yet modish, calf-length lace dress with matching veil of mantilla-like lace.

**CONTEMPLATING THE NAVAL** *(right)* Catherine Walker's double-breasted white/navy pinstripe coat-dress was first worn to visit a naval base in La Spezia, when Graham Smith's perky sailor-style "doughboy" hat, a.k.a. Bob Cap, provided the perfect finishing touch to an outfit with a nautical flavor. It is seen here on a trip to Portland, Australia, in October 1985.

**JAPANESE IF YOU PLEASE** *(above)* That was the thinking behind this choice—as a tribute to her host country, Diana chose Japanese designer Yuki's vivid blue, Erte-inspired, Fortuny-pleated, long dinner dress with bugle-beaded yoke, echoed with a diamond design at waist. This was the only occasion she wore anything by Yuki, and his one-and-only would go under the hammer and raise $25,300 in the Christie's auction.

**LA VIE EN ROSE** *(right)* Once again showing off the bare shoulder, as well as her favorite color combination of black and red, Diana wore Catherine Walker's black taffeta balldress, printed with misty roses, on an official visit to Paris in 1988. It was to fetch $27,600 in Christie's auction.

**DIPLOMATIC DI** *(left)* A visit to West Germany called for a complementary label—the Princess was an Escada aficionado, so problem solved. She wore their yellow/black windowpane checked coat with a matching turban by Philip Somerville.

**THE FILM STAR LOOK** *(below left)* In a style reminiscent of Grace Kelly, Diana attended the 1987 Cannes Film Festival in this strapless, pale blue, chiffon dress by Catherine Walker.

When in Japan, Diana paid homage to the country with a nod to the East—she wore a dress by Japanese designer, Yuki, for a banquet in Tokyo in May 1986. This was a long, royal blue, bugle-beaded number—not one of her most flattering.

Murray Arbeid's "Lady of Spain confection"—a flamboyant, Stendhal-esque bi-colored, black, velvet-bodiced long evening gown, falling onto an asymmetric, flounced, flamenco-style scarlet taffeta skirt, worn on an official visit to that country in 1987, was both a triumph and an accolade.

For Germany, it was Diana's favorite label, the German Escada, whose yellow and black windowpane checked coat she wore on a visit to the country in November 1987, accessorized with matching bi-colored turban, and black suede knee boots. Diana was exemplary at looking the part, as well as saluting the occasion with a dress-code that paid a compliment to her hosts.

Channel-crossing called for Chanel-style French dressing—a red, double-breasted bouclé coat with signature gilt buttons and forage cap

**FRENCH POLISH** *(left)* Total Chanel was the order of the day from the top of her perky little forage cap with black feather trim to the signature quilted chain handled bag, taking in the scarlet bouclé, double-breasted, brass-buttoning V-necked coat and collarless white crêpe pintucked blouse. In top-to-toe Chanel, the Princess chose to salute France on a visit to Paris by wearing its most celebrated fashion label.

**ROYAL HUSSAR** (above) The military influence is to the fore in Catherine Walker's black velvet/red crêpe, braid trimmed, ankle-skimming skirt.

**JOIN THE MAJORETTE SET** (right) Occasion dressing was her forte, and when the Princess was poised to go on parade at Sandhurst Military Academy, she appeared in Catherine Walker's stylish gold-braided, cream wool suit with epaulettes and asymmetrical skirt, set off with Graham Smith's high-crowned straw hat.

attending the film premier of *Steel Magnolias* in 1990.

For her trip to Lahore, Pakistan, she respected the custom of the country by wearing the shalwar kameez; an official visit to Saudi Arabia inspired a long, formal, cream silk dinner-dress, again by Catherine Walker—long-sleeved and high-necked, it was in keeping with the country's custom, while the gold falcon embroidery paid homage to the ruling royal house.

For a tour of India in 1992, a long, rose-pink wild silk evening dress with matching bolero jacket, designed by the omnipresent Walker, featured embroidery on both the bodice and jacket. Decorated with green, star-shaped sequins, gold glass beads, and gold braid, it was redolent of Mughal embroidery, again a mark of respect for the Princess' Indian hosts.

**SAY IT WITH FLOWERS** *(above)* Albeit embroidered steel magnolias! The title of the film that was being premiered that night provided the inspiration behind the gold and simulated pearl floral embroidery on Catherine Walker's burgundy velvet jacket—a variation on a man's tailcoat theme. First seen in 1990, it also went to Korea in 1992 and ended up in the Christie's auction, where it raised $26,450.

**SHALWAR KAMEEZ, DESTINED TO PLEASE** *(above left)* Acknowledging indigenous customs and *couleur locale* was the POW's maxim, and favorite designer Catherine Walker always did her homework for the trips. Here, Diana wears Walker's powder blue, raw silk shalwar kameez for a trip to Lahore in June 1997.

**BLAIR'S FLAIR** *(far left)* Pagodalike flounces on the skirt of this navy and white silk print dress by Alistair Blair provided a nod toward the East, set off with lattice brimmed straw hat by Philip Somerville and two-tone shoes.

by Chanel designer Karl Lagerfeld, worn with a classic CC logo'd chain-handled, quilted shoulder bag, was Diana's choice for a fitting tribute to her hosts, for her arrival at Orly Airport in 1988.

For her visit to Sandhurst Military Academy, in April 1987, Diana wore a white drum majorette suit, with gold-braid-trimmed jacket and asymmetric, back-slit skirt, set off with a pert, high-crowned straw hat—a fitting fashion uniform for going on parade.

A Black Watch tartan dress with lace collar was seemly for a visit to Bute, in Scotland, in August 1987, and it appeared again at the Braemar Highland Games the following year.

On a visit to Thailand in 1988, the Princess picked a silk print dress with knee-length, flounced flirty skirt, reminiscent of a pagoda—another reference to the East.

Beaded flowers of pearl and gold-leaf thread bloomed on Catherine Walker's dinner-dress and tailcoat of burgundy velvet, a witty choice for

# Personal hallmarks

There were a number of looks and themes that the Princess espoused, such as tartan, nautical, military, and androgynous. She also loved spots.

Tartan proved a natural choice for the Braemar Highland Games. For her debut at this event, in September 1981, Diana chose a Caroline Charles rust, brown, and black mid-length plaid dress with stand-up collar, looped buttons, and braid trim, worn with a black tam o'shanter. This dress became a constant in her wardrobe, cropping up with different shirts.

A trip to Bute, in Scotland, in August 1987, saw a prettied-up version of clan chic—by David Sassoon, in classic Black Watch tartan, it was lent a Romantic feel with a girly, white, antique-look lace puritan collar and cuffs. Again it had the mid-long, pleated skirt. For switching on the London Christmas lights in 1993, we saw an altogether more sophisticated play on plaidery: another David Sassoon, this time in Royal Stewart tartan, translated into a long-line, double-breasted jacket with contrasting black velvet trim, worn over a black velvet pencil skirt.

Tartan was reeled out by night, too. For dancing at Balmoral, Diana had Catherine Walker make her a long-sleeved ballgown with black velvet bodice, punctuated with scarlet velvet piping, falling onto a full, petticoated skirt of green, black, and red silk taffeta plaid.

Diana loved the "smoking suit," and tuxedos in various guises proved

**ROYAL STEWART** *(above and sketch, right)*
A tartan interpretation of a long-line, double-breasted jacket with velvet trim to match the pencil skirt. "She thought straight skirts were very sophisticated," says designer David Sassoon.

**TARTAN GETS THE SOFT TOUCH** *(above)*
A mid-length pleated, skirted long-sleeved Black Watch tartan dress, by David Sassoon, is prettied up with Victorian lace puritan style collar.

**THE REEL THING** *(left)* This long formal dress was designed by Catherine Walker for Scottish dancing at Balmoral. The Elizabethan-style pointed bodice in black velvet falls onto a full skirt of green, black, and red silk taffeta plaid.

popular in the royal wardrobe. Diana's first venture into the androgynous look, ground-breaking in royal fashion terms, was an ivory DJ with satin lapels, worn with contrasting black slacks. Designed by Margaret Howell, this was chosen as appropriate "cool" gear for a rock concert in Birmingham in February 1984, when the Princess was newly pregnant with Harry.

In February 1987, a zesty orange satin bellhop jacket by Jasper Conran, worn with black satin bow

April 1988. The wittiest take on the tuxedo theme was Victor Edelstein's spoof tailcoat-dress, a long, slinky velvet dress faced with contrast black ribbed silk with three glitzy paste

DI'S WAY WITH A DJ *(left)* A stricter variation on the theme, worn with wing-collared shirt and black satin bow tie by Catherine Walker. A frozen-pea-green waistcoat from the man's store Hackett layered up underneath the DJ lent an unexpected explosion of color to an otherwise classic, man-tailored, tuxedo suit.

Ties were another of the occasional accessories that Diana borrowed from the boys. There was the celebrated Escada elephant-print style worn to visit her sister-in-law at St. Mary's Hospital after the birth of Victoria's son Louis. Robina Ziff, who owns the Escada store in London's Bond Street, where Diana bought the outfit, recalls: "I shall never forget the elephant episode. We had the whole of Fleet Street banging down the doors. At the time, I was asked to go on a television program, as every-one was saying that Diana looked like an "Essex Girl" in the outfit, which I couldn't do, as it would have been an indictment on all my clients.

"So I decided that I would have to telephone the Princess and warn the palace that there had been

## "The only way I can stop them is to put a sack over my head!"

DIANA, PRINCESS OF WALES

tie, appeared at the ballet in Portugal. Diana lent an injection of color to her best bib'n'tucker with the addition of an apple-green waistcoat. The DJ was by Catherine Walker and the eclectic waistcoat hailed from Hackett, a men's store. This was the Princess' put-together for a charity evening held at Wembley Greyhound Stadium in

buttons. Being totally feminine and sensuous in style, it was perfectly politically correct for the 1989 premier of *Dangerous Liaisons*.

something of a catastrophe," said Robina, casting her mind back to the event. "I told them that we had had all these newspaper people saying

**THE UNFORGETTABLE ELEPHANT** *(above)*
Thanks to the Princess, the Ele' jacket was a
best-seller. Robina Ziff, Escada's Bond Street
store owner, has been unable to part with hers,
as, for her, it is something of which royal
memories are made.

**MOOD MILITARY** *(left)* This was a favorite
Catherine Walker that enjoyed many airings—the
scarlet wool suit, which has a fitted, cutaway
military-style, brass-buttoning jacket, is worn over
a matching, short pencil skirt.

**PRINCESS ON PARADE** *(left below)* Cassis-
colored suit with military-style, brass-buttoning
jacket and black velvet trademark stand collar, by
Turkish designer Rifat Ozbek.

hurtful things about the POW. I
wanted to assure them that we were
not the ones responsible. Ten
minutes later the phone rang and it
was Diana's dresser to tell us that she
had informed her boss and had been
instructed to tell us please, not to
worry. Apparently Diana had said
'The only way I can stop them is to
put a sack over my head!'"

The military mood was marched
out for a visit to Little London,
Hampshire, England, in 1988, in the
form of Catherine Walker's pillarbox red suit, double-breasted and
brass-buttoned, with a finely fitted,
cutaway mess-style jacket over a
shortish pencil skirt.

Two other examples of soldier-
style that were paraded by the
Princess were made for her by
Turkish designer Rifat Ozbek. The
first of these was a black cherry-
colored suit—an officer's jacket with
contrast black velvet stand collar and
brass buttons—and the second was
the Ozbek suit that appeared at
Caen, France, in September 1987,
made of scarlet wool with a contrasting black collar, trimmed with
military buttons.

All the nice girls love the sailor look, and Diana was no exception. The initial engagement picture with the Queen marked the first sighting of Di's sailor-girl style—one that would prove recurrent in classic navy and white or softer, silky brights.

For a visit to Nottingham Hospital with her boys, Diana went for this nautical theme with a short-sleeved navy dress featuring one of her favorite touches—contrasting white collar and cuffs and a double row of baby brass buttons on the skirt. Navy court shoes decorated with orange polka dots were an unexpected touch.

The most relaxed prototype of this look is a rarely-seen picture taken by photographer Gemma Levine, in 1995, in which Diana is photographed off-duty in an ivory washed silk sailor shirt with navy collar and cuff trim, by the French label Equipment.

**SPOT THOSE SOCKS** *(above)* Coordinating polka-dotted, mid-calf-length, pleated skirt and ankle sox, worn with red, low-heeled pumps, lend a '50s co-ed campus feel to this Mondi outfit, spotted at polo in the summer of 1986.

**NAUTI-MUMMY** *(opposite, far left)* The POW combines two of her favorite trademarks in a single navy sailor-collared dress with white matelot collar and sleeve trim.

**MATELOT LOOK** *(opposite)* A more relaxed informal slant to the sailor yarn—the Princess captured in camera, looking cool and relaxed in ivory washed silk long-sleeved shirt with nautical navy and cream stripe collar and cuff trim by the Paris label Equipment, purchased by the Princess from favorite Knightsbridge store, Harvey Nichols. Diana loved this shirt—her first such design wore out and she replaced it with a second one. Paired with navy pants and well-manicured royal tootsies.

**FORMAL SPOTS** *(right)* Polka dots and white trim work in tandem for Catherine Walker's turquoise and white dress with contrast white droopy collar, buttons, and pocket trim. The dress features a kick-pleated hemline, and the broad-brimmed hat re-echoes the bicolored theme.

Diana was dotty about spots and polka dots, as in the case of the ubiquitous, much-altered black and white Edelstein dress that graced many occasions, usually race meetings.

Her most striking spotty outfit was a white and red, coin-spotted, V-necked silk dress with exaggerated shoulder line that she wore to visit the Nija Palace in Kyoto, Japan, in May 1986. It had a cummerbunded waist and was accessorized with a graphic red hat, matching shoes, and a single row of pearls at the neck. Due credit for this must go to Missie Crockett of Tatters.

A month later, spots were worn more casually, but nonetheless to striking effect. White and red spotted ankle sox, coordinated with red pumps, provided the foot finish to a Mondi outfit of matching mid-length, pleated skirt worn with white-ringed red Sloppy Jo sweater over a white skirt. Kind of cutesy, girly.

You couldn't miss the Princess at sister-in-law Fergie's wedding in July 1986. For the occasion, Diana chose a turquoise and black polka-dot silk dress, V-necked, and cinched with dramatic black inset corset-belt and a matching, bicolored tricorne-style hat. A stylish choice for one of the best-dressed wedding guests, without stealing the bride's thunder.

A Catherine Walker turquoise and white, long-sleeved, silk dress with polka dots that matched the buttons and droopy white collar, with a pleated skirt, worn in March 1989, seemed far too mumsy and sedate for Diana, but it proved to be a calm before the storm.

**SHEER WINDOW** *(right)* A panel of sheer floral lace, overlaid on flesh-colored chiffon, makes a provocative exit-line on a simple long navy floral dress by Catherine Walker.

**STRAPPING BACK** *(below right)* Redolent of a racing swimsuit, and making the most of her well-worked-out physique, this beaded beauty by Jacques Azagury was worn by Diana on the night of her "Panorama" TV interview in July 1996.

In Diana's case, her exit was often as memorable as her entrance. She once said: "When I wear a backless dress, I find that most people don't know where to put their hands."

One of her most memorable about-turns was a long-sleeved, ruby crushed velvet dress by Catherine Walker, worn for the premier of Spielberg's *Back To The Future*, with a rope of pearls, casually knotted and dangling down Diana's back to highlight the exposed V-décolleté back.

For a visit to London's Serpentine Gallery in July 1996, Diana wore a long, bias-cut dress with sensuous cross-back straps. Towards the end of her life, for a charity dinner to support the victims of landmines, Diana looked sublime in the simplest, most stunning of dresses. Worn in Washington in June 1997, this was a flame-red sheath with deep, décolleté V-back, exposing a golden-brown tan.

The year of her death marked Diana's finest fashion year to date. For the premier of Lord Attenborough's film *In Love and War* in February 1997, she wore another volte-face stunner—a long navy floral lace sheath dress with a subtle

**PEARLY PRINCESS** *(above right)* A knotted river of pearls flows down the deep V-décolletage of Catherine Walker's witty take on the premier of *Back to the Future*, for which it was designed.

**BACK LOOKS** *(right)* A taffeta bustle-back, caught with a black velvet bow, provides the exit-line on this cocktail dress by Victor Edelstein.

**DARING PLUNGE** *(far right)* Jacques Azagury's flame sheath dress proves that back interest can be just as sensuous as being up-front about it.

**SHOULDER SHOW** *(top)* Worn on a visit to Brazil in 1991, Catherine Walker's one-sleeved sari-dress fetched over $26,000 at Christie's auction.

**EARLY HINT** *(above)* In 1985, Bruce Oldfield's long peacock silk dress, with its asymmetric neckline, gave a foretaste of the look to come.

**SMOULDERING SHOULDER** *(above left)* The single sexy shoulder appears here in Versace's blue satin sheath with a single sliver of gilt strap.

insert of sheer gossamer flesh and navy lace at the back.

Blessed with a great pair of shoulders, Diana also maximized this part of her anatomy. From the spectacular one-shouldered, white Hachi dress that stunned Down Under in 1983, the "smouldering shoulder" became synonymous with Diana. This toga style was first seen in 1982 with Bruce Oldfield's electric blue ruffled, slant-shouldered crêpe-de-chine long evening dress worn to the Guildhall in London.

A memorable, floor-sweeping, aquamarine organza evening dress, one-shouldered and caught with a bow, falling onto a dropped-waist skirt was yet another Oldfield design. A cobalt blue, one-shouldered column dress caught with a signature shoulder strap on the high-set slant neckline, worn in October 1996, hailed from Italian designer, Versace.

LIKE ANY NORMAL young girl Diana loved to shop anonymously, popping in to places spontaneously and, preferably, incognito. Being left alone to browse was one of her great joys.

If the Princess had her Frock-Stars, then Simon Wilson, of Butler & Wilson, costume jewellers to the "Beautiful People," was to be her Rock-Star. His London's Fulham Road store, a veritable Aladdin's cave of glittering prizes, was heaven to Diana, a total antithesis to the Crown Jewels, with which she was over-endowed.

The likes of Catherine Deneuve, Charlotte Rampling, Faye Dunaway, Marie Helvin, Lauren Hutton, Shakira Caine, Jerry Hall, Twiggy, Sophie Ward, Marisa

# Butler &
# WILSON

**GALACTIC CHIC** *(above)* The rumor mill insisted that these star and moon drop diamanté earrings, worn to a desert picnic in Saudi Arabia in 1986, were a gift received on her visit to the Gulf States, but Di—and Butler & Wilson—had everyone fooled.

Berenson, Talisa Soto, Ali McGraw, and Dame Edna Everidge have all graced Simon's billboards over the years. Wearing his costume jewelry, these celebrities epitomized the mood of the moment. Conspicuous by her very absence is the most famous, most photographed face of them all, Butler & Wilson's most celebrated customer—Diana, Princess of Wales.

Simon Wilson first met the POW in 1984: "She lived up to every expectation. She had that wonderful presence; she was tall, had beautiful eyes, and this incredible natural-ness," he remembers. "The beauty of her coming here was that you didn't interfere; the great thing was to actually leave her alone like a normal customer. She'd come in very

informally; the bodyguard would just stand aside. It was her interaction with other customers—'what do you think?'—that was such fun. They would turn around, and there she would be," he recalls.

"I think that she was obviously guided on clothes, but with accessories, she decided for herself," believes Wilson. "My all-time favorite piece of jewelry was her big sapphire and diamond choker. She used costume jewellery to customize her clothes, and to add wit and individuality to her wardrobe."

Diana's first piece of *faux bijouterie* from B. & W. was a pair of crystal and heart bow earrings. "It gave her a kick that they were fake," explains Simon.

**FAKE SNAKE** *(above)* A striking black bead and gemstoned serpent-pin—another little nugget from costume jeweler Butler & Wilson—is espied slithering along the lapel of Diana's Jasper Conran black tuxedo jacket.

In May 1986, Diana caused mayhem at a rock concert in Vancouver, when she appeared dressed in a black tuxedo with white ruffled shirt from Jasper Conran. A black-bead and gemstone snake was espied slithering up the jacket's lapel.

Prince Charles bought his wife a Maltese Cross Order from Marshall Field in Chicago, a snip at $75. Diana pinned this piece onto the center of the black velvet bodice of Murray Arbeid's memorable, dramatic bicolored red flamenco-

**STARBURST** *(above)* The Princess' tresses are elegantly upswept at the back of her head, and caught with a dramatic diamanté starburst clip for a fashion show in Sydney, Australia, in January 1988.

**MISSION ACCOMPLISHED** *(left)* For a film premier, the POW, who loved a wind-up, wore a costume piece that everyone took for the real thing—the Maltese Cross pin.

skirted dress, for a premier of *The Mission* in October 1986.

"She also wore a huge diamanté star at the back of her hair on one occasion, bought from us," recalls Simon. "The other famous story was when she went to Saudi Arabia, and everyone believed that she had been given this galactic gift," chortles Wilson. "It was a crescent moon-and-star earring, and tongues were wagging. The whole world was talking about this gift of gold and diamond earrings that cost $37!"

# chapter five
# cover girl

"Imagine having to go to a
wedding every day as the bride.
That's what it's like."

DIANA, PRINCESS OF WALES

# New Directions

> ## "Photography reshaped her image."
>
> ANWAR HUSSEIN, PHOTOGRAPHER

BY THE MID- TO LATE EIGHTIES, the Princess had grown enormously in stature. Diana was at last going places, spreading her wings, globe-trotting on foreign tours and official visits, becoming acknowledged as a British ambassadress, and, as such, one of the country's major assets. She has, for the most part, abandoned the New Romantic and purely pretty, prissy touches of her early make-believe phase in favor of a more sophisticated style.

"Imagine having to go to a wedding every day as the bride. That's what it's like," she quipped.

Diana has sharpened up her act; she has edited her designer stable, confining it to those best suited to her royal role.

The key players at the court of the Princess, then, are pared down to Catherine Walker, Victor Edelstein, Murray Arbeid, and Bruce Oldfield, at least for Di-by-night.

We now begin to see more of Dynasty Di, the glamorous Princess, as she starts to enjoy being center-stage, even glorying in her new role as Cover-Girl, rather than Shy Di'ing away from the limelight.

Royal photographer, Anwar Hussein is on record as saying: "Photography, more than the written word, reshaped her image."

And she certainly socked it to the paparazzi, responding to these flash bulbs by flashing back.

As designer Victor Edelstein says: "Her style had evolved from those puritan-collared dresses to inevitably simpler and simpler tastes as she got older."

Edelstein created that definitive midnight-blue velvet dress the Princess wore to a State Dinner hosted by the Reagans in 1995, and she certainly wowed the White House. Undoubtedly "The Dress of That Year," this is the one that danced the night away with dishy John Travolta and that came to be dubbed the "Travolta" dress.

Probably the most famous dress in Diana's entire wardrobe, it re-emerged for a trip to Germany in December 1987, and made a further appearance at the premier of *Wall Street* in April 1988.

It has to be said that this was a knockout dress, dramatic in style, regal in fabric, and it showed off Diana's stunning shoulder-line to perfection. The dress also had a slight sweep of costume drama, being Edwardian in inspiration.

Who could have predicted that this particular dress would be the star-turn of the Christie's auction and go

**VICTOR EDELSTEIN** (*above*) The man behind the "Travolta" dress, Victor Edelstein, who has now reinvented himself as a painter and lives in Spain.

**HALTER NECK** (*previous page*) Black beads embellish the plunge neckline of Walker's velvet dinner dress, worn to Versailles in 1994.

under the hammer for "the princessly sum" of $222,500! Some revenue-raiser. It has certainly made its contribution to charity.

"Of course I am pleased, though I never went to the auction," recalls Victor, now retired from the fashion arena. He casts his mind back, to the first time he met the Princess. "Anna Harvey of *Vogue* recommended me to the POW; it was just after she'd had Prince William. The first dress that I made for her was a maternity dress; and it was sight unseen. I then took it in and transformed it into a normal evening dress. I can't even remember what color it was. I think that it was pink, but I never saw Diana till afterwards."

"I worked with Diana for 11 years or more and I must have made her about 60-70 pieces. Possibly I was No. 2," he suggests modestly. "The things that she chose from the collection were exclusive inside the royal family, and if I designed something special for her, that too, was exclusive. We never kept a toile for the Princess, as she was model size, so it was never difficult," he says.

"Her personality was inspirational. She was so nice and

thoughtful. Of course I am constantly being asked about the POW, but there is nothing extraordinary to say."

Edelstein cites as his most memorable pieces, "the velvet dress that she danced in with John Travolta; the ivory one with the bolero that she wore in Paris; the black strapless velvet sheath with the three diamond buttons that went to *Dangerous Liaisons'* first night—those three are most meaningful to me. Then there was the short outfit that she wore to the ballet in Germany," he recalls.

"I know that the Princess favored the dark blue velvet dress and the ivory one in the sale," confirms Victor.

Like his peers, Edelstein found the Princess totally charming, disarming, and delightful. "She would always come down to the front door to say goodbye, rather than just say her farewells downstairs, and she would

**C'EST SI BON** *(left)* The "Travolta" dress was such a success, it re-emerged on a trip to Germany in December 1987, and made a further appearance at the premier of *Wall Street* in April 1988. The designer's working sketch *(far left)* illustrates the detailed draping, caught with a bow at the side.

**WHITE HOUSE FEVER** *(above)* A radiant Nancy Reagan looks on as Diana dances the night away with Travolta at the White House in "That Dress."

always send me a birthday card, sometimes a present. She would come to the rehearsals of my shows to avoid the press; she would talk to my dressmakers—take the time to remember their names, which made their day. She was very appreciative and she had this incredible gift—she would talk to people for three or four minutes and give them her total attention, which made her visits," enthuses Edelstein.

Other seismic styles from this designer include the long-tiered black lace "Goya-esque" dress, layered over magenta silk, to lend the illusion of bronze, with short, cap sleeves, falling onto a flounced lace skirt, worn on the same German trip as the "Travolta" dress; a fuchsia-draped, cowl-backed long silk, '30s-inspired evening dress, first sighted in Japan in November 1990; again at the opera, and once more in London for the charity Help The Hospice. It is easy to spot the favorites, because they

**TWO FACES OF BLACK LACE** The back view of the bodice of Victor Edelstein's black silk lace number *(above)* reveals the delicate intricacy of the lace. The Goya-inspired tiered dress *(right)*, worn here with a double strand of pearls, was to fetch over $25,000 at Christie's auction.

## "A real-life fairy-story that had a very sad ending."

MURRAY ARBEID

are always worn on several important occasions. Such as Victor's long, ultra-formal strapless dinner dress in oyster Duchesse satin. It had an elaborately embroidered bodice of carnation and birds in simulated pearls, with paste and bugle beads, etched in gold by Hurel, with a matching bolero jacket. This was worn at a state banquet hosted by President and Mme

Mitterand at the Elysée Palace, in 1988, and then again at the Wintergarden, in New York.

Murray Arbeid's name is synonymous with the Stendhal-esque red and black flamenco designs, and the fabulous galactic embroidered, strapless, midnight-blue, silk tulle, ballerina-length dance dress with dropped waist.

**THAT COLOR AGAIN** This was another of the Princess' Edelstein favorites—his fuchsia-pink silk evening dress with its inverted wrap-over front pleat *(left)*. From behind we see the cowled, draped back, falling onto a long skirt that fans into a tailed, mermaiden hemline *(above)*. This '30s-inspired evening dress was first sighted in Japan in November 1989, and again in London at a dinner for the charity Help The Hospice.

Like Edelstein, Murray Arbeid, is no longer a frock-star. I guess that once you've made for the POW, you cannot aspire to anything higher.

Now retired and living in Suffolk, England, the designer idolized Diana, whom he met a long time ago after a show featuring British designers. "The POW picked up on some of the clothes from that show. I was told which dresses she liked; I prepared them and took them along to KP and fitted them on her.

"My first impression of the Princess was that she was one of the nicest people one could ever meet—very understanding, pleasant, simple, lovely, just perfect in every way—it would be impossible to say anything untoward about her," he insists.

"There is so much over-exposure about her. It is just a real-life fairy-story that had a very sad ending," he stresses. "Every moment that I spent with that woman was an absolute delight," he says emphatically.

"Take this example. She asked me to make a bolero: 'I need it in a great hurry—I know that you are doing your collection at the moment—you are showing in a week's time,' she said. I didn't tell her, she just knew," remembers the designer.

"I suppose I did about eight evening dresses for Diana. The red and black flamenco one and the navy star-spangled tulle one are the most famous—Snowdon took three publicity pictures for the Christie's auction and they were really very nice indeed," says Arbeid.

Murray's red flamenco number fetched just over $25,000; the

stunning navy blue strapless galactic tulle, $48,300.

Diana chose his formal, ivory, taffeta-skirted, long evening dress, falling from a bodice of lace with scalloped high neckline, to wear at a dinner at the British Embassy in November 1985.

"The fact that one got to make clothes for the most famous woman in the world, was a huge, huge benefit, and I was justifiably proud and felt privileged to be part of the scene."

Murray adds, "The Princess was as popular as she was because of the person that she was. It may sound

like saccharine, but it isn't meant that way. She was just a marvelous person, and there is nothing else to say about her. Once, during a fitting, I knocked over a box of pins and we were both down on our hands and knees picking them up. I didn't know her before she married, but I found her a perfectly lovely, natural person. British design in the '80s was really going somewhere and, by an incredible stroke of good fortune, we had her as a figurehead.

"People say, 'Oh how could anybody be so perfect?' Well we had some marvelous ballerinas, too. You did get shining stars, and Diana was a shining star for people growing up in the '80s. I was lucky to have lived through Margot Fonteyn and through the Princess of Wales' era. What else could a man ask?" sighs Arbeid reflectively.

Bruce Oldfield was still very much the golden boy, and made a number of striking dresses for the Princess around this time, notably the gold Fortuny-pleated, bare triangle-backed evening dress for the charity dinner for Barnardos at Grosvenor House in March 1985. He also made the celebrated silk one-shouldered, long, drop-waisted kingfisher dress that Diana accessorized to stunning effect by using her Queen Mary choker as a headband, as she was swept happily across the dance floor by Prince Charles at the Southern Cross Hotel, in Melbourne, Australia, in 1985.

Bruce Oldfield also made a couple of "Dynasty Di" dresses for her—a scarlet one with padded shoulders and Odeon-curtain-style draping at the waist for that same Australian trip. The Lady-in-Red dress, worn at the Gold and Red Charity Ball later that year, was his, as was the off-the-shoulder, purple ruched confection.

Deep V-necklines were an Oldfield signature, featuring on a cobalt blue and fuchsia pink long evening dress, with tea-cozy effect elbow-length sleeves, and "POW-er" shoulders in the Princess' favorite polka-dot print. Another stunner was a long, V-necked velvet dress, stark and dramatic, worn for the first night of *Les Misérables*.

The deep, roll collar was a favorite detail of many of Diana's jackets at the time, and Oldfield designed her a striking white cotton suit with this neckline, piped in contrasting black, draped at the side

with contrast buttons that were echoed on the knee-length pencil skirt. First seen with a two-tone hat for a day at the horse races in Melbourne, the same suit was to reappear in June of the same year, this time worn more casually to attend a polo match.

Towards the late '80s, the Princess became more cosmopolitan in her taste, extending her patronage to European labels—German, French, and Italian in particular.

One such label was Escada, whose yellow and black "Paddington Bear"-style coat she wore to Germany.

Were it not for a Louis Feraud fashion show, held for the charity Birthright at the London Palladium, the Princess would probably never have met Robina Ziff and started wearing the Escada label.

"It was as a result of meeting her on that occasion that she came to my Escada shop," recalls Robina. "A couple of weeks later, we sent her a catalogue. Shortly afterward, she came through the door unannounced with her bodyguard, as became her wont," says Robina. "She became a loyal customer since that initial meeting. I am often away on buying trips, so it would always be a manager who looked after her, or her dresser, Fay Appleby, would telephone to say, 'she can't come over, could you send some things, please.'

"When she did find the time to come in personally, she would, because she loved being like an ordinary shopper. She loved mingling with the public. It was all part of her wanting to be normal. I remember one time she was going down to our VIP room for some fittings; she was just walking downstairs and a builder was walking up, and this navvy bumped straight into her, and nearly fell down the stairs with astonishment," she remembers.

"Another time she had been to some event at Great Ormond Street Hospital. She came running in saying, 'I have escaped, I've been to Great Ormond Street and felt like doing some shopping on my own.' On another occasion, she intended to wear an Escada turquoise silk summer dress, and as she was getting

**MADE FOR DANCING** *(above)* Bruce Oldfield's silver lamé spangled red silk chiffon dress, with a hip-length draped bodice, appeared appropriately at the film premier of *Hot Shots*, in 1991.

**PRINCESS OF OZ** *(left)* Dancing the night away with Charles, in Melbourne in 1985, Diana lends this outfit a personal touch with her Queen Mary choker, worn as a headband, to stunning effect.

into it, the zip broke. She panicked. We had a phone call, collected said dress, repaired the zip, sent it straight back, and HRH called to say that she couldn't thank us enough for doing this so promptly," says Robina.

"Diana was always absolutely 'correct' if we sent her clothes on 'spec' or from the catalogue—if there was something unsuitable, it came back promptly the following morning; she would never hang on to clothes that she didn't want, unlike other members of the Royal

**EVER FASHION RIGHT—GRAPHIC BLACK & WHITE** *(right)* The deep roll collar was a favorite detail on many of the POW's jackets at the time and featured on Oldfield's striking white cotton suit, piped in contrasting black, the jacket having padded power shoulders, caught and draped on the hip with gold buttons; the navy skirt echoes the white of the jacket with its boutonnage. It was worn with a bicolored hat for a day at the races in Melbourne, in 1985.

Family, where sometimes the clothes didn't even come back!

"When the boys were in nursery school, Diana would drop in, in jeans and boots; she'd come with a driver, do some shopping, then suddenly she'd look at her watch and say, 'I have to go and pick up the boys.'"

would come in, go through the rails with Ken Wharfe (her bodyguard) and ask his opinion—'Ken, what do you think of this, do you like it?'

"David Sassoon and I shared a joke concerning the POW. David and I were due to meet for lunch at San Lorenzo, but I had a client who

## "She loved being like an ordinary shopper."

ROBINA ZIFF

"She wore an Escada outfit the first day that she took William to school—a red skirt and an emblem sweater. That sweater had gold crowns on it, and when she saw that, she simply had to have it. She thought it would be a laugh because of the gold crowns. She

kept delaying me. I actually arrived 45 minutes later than planned. When I reached San Lorenzo, there was David sitting with Princess Diana, whose date—her brother—was also late. Coincidentally, we were wearing exactly the same Escada outfit—a

**TAKING A SHINE TO SATIN** *(left)* For Michael Jackson's concert in the summer of 1988, the Princess picked up on the key fabric of the season—satin. Catherine Walker's translation of the sensuous cloth into a pencil-skirted suit with a fitted cutaway jacket over a contrasting black camisole top was totally appropriate and sufficiently princessy for a pop concert.

**ALL WHITE ON THE NIGHT** *(opposite page and far left)* For a Birthright Benefit at the London Palladium, the Princess went for white—Zandra Rhodes' gauzy, fairy-tale lace dress with a high V-neck, long sheer sleeves, and satin waist sash, worn with single pearl choker at the neck. The Zandra dress was later recycled and passed on to Princess Margaret's daughter, Lady Sarah Armstrong-Jones.

Black Watch tartan suit. It was quite a hot day, and the Princess was dressed in the jacket, shirt, and skirt, the entire ensemble, right down to the matching tartan shoes. I walked in and thought 'Oh my God.' I had to react quickly, so I shrugged my jacket off so the similarity wouldn't be so obvious," remembers Robina.

"It was hysterical, and she just laughed back."

Mrs. Ziff confirms Diana's yo-yoing weight. "We watched her fluctuating in size considerably, and actually we became very concerned. Basically, she was 8-10, because being 5' 11" tall, she took up the size in the height and length. She was getting thinner and thinner—at one stage, the bones in her back stuck out so much that it was actually quite scary—for someone to be 5' 11" and take a size 6, is very, very thin," comments Robina.

The Princess was becoming decidedly more adventurous in her dress, and at last her hemlines were becoming visibly shorter. She was also putting on the shine.

A shiny, sunflower yellow, satin skirt-suit, with a double-breasted, cutaway jacket, accessorized with contrasting black, by Catherine Walker, cropped up at a Michael Jackson concert in June 1988. The previous year, Diana had worn a black satin jacket, red and black striped blouse, and lacquer-red leather slacks to *Phantom of the Opera*. The Princess craved the Continental touch. And why not? A beautiful young woman such as Diana deserved the pick of international labels.

One of her favorites was a navy, military-style, double-breasted, brass-buttoning jacket, paired with knee-skimming pinstripe suit from Yves Saint-Laurent's Rive Gauche.

Real fur was not deemed fitting for a princess, but faking it can be even more dramatic, as Diana proved on a visit to Germany in Bella Pollen's oatmeal bathrobe coat. Deeply banded with contrast black faux fur on the shawl collar and cuffs, the coat was worn with a matching beret and knee-high boots.

There was "Dutiful Di" and "Off-Duty Di," but because we tended to see more images of the former, when the Princess did appear in her casual, more laid-back looks, it was distinctly refreshing. Two such examples, both taken at Windsor Polo matches, sum up the mood—Diana in a pair of pink and white gingham trousers, teamed with a white cotton shirt with rolled up sleeves and flat pumps; Diana in pastel blue dungarees, white T-shirt, and classic navy-blue blazer.

The Emanuels enjoyed something of a revival on Diana's Saudi tour, their most notable dress being a bicolored, monochromatic-bodiced dress in Duchesse satin, caught with a Regency-striped chocolate box bow at the waist.

But it was Catherine Walker who was starting to emerge as a tour-de-force in Diana's wardrobe. She could mix the royal cocktail like no other. Walker's soaraway successes included the powder-blue, contrast-piped nanny-coats worn by the young Princes to synchronize with Mummy's (an idea conceived by Diana in conjunction with Walker); a navy velvet evening dress with sheer lace yoke; a long bicolored, fluid, cream and salmon-pink silk Empire-line dress; and the fuchsia, purple-stoled, draped long chiffon Thailand dress.

Walker had a repertoire that was all-embracing—she could turn her hand to virtually anything and nothing seemed too great a challenge, whether it was a tailored suit, the simplest dress that relied on cut and drape, or the most intricately beaded evening gown for a state occasion.

VOGUE

DEC £2·50

the year of
**dance**
A CHRISTMAS CELEBRATION

9 770262 213029

**BATHROBE COAT** *(top)* A roomy bathrobe coat, in blonde cashmere and wool mix with faux beaver shawl collar and deep cuffs by Arabella Pollen provided the chameleonic classic for traveling on official trips or wearing off-duty.

**THE PRINCESS WE KNEW AND LOVED** *(above)* Off-duty weekending at Windsor polo, a casual Diana is caught in camera in sheer white shirt with rolled up sleeves partnered by red and white gingham pants and flat pumps.

**DRAMATIC IN BLACK AND WHITE** *(above and left)* Diana wore a striking Duchesse satin dress, with two-toned bodice falling onto a full white satin skirt, to a state banquet with King Fahd, in Riyadh, Saudi Arabia, in November 1986. The original croquis for the design by the Emanuels shows the force behind the idea.

DIANA HAD THE CREAM of the designer crop at her disposal, yet it was a shy Frenchwoman who became her fashion mentor. Of all the royal frock-makers, Catherine Walker is the one who stayed the course. She made the lion's share of Diana's wardrobe (to say 1,000 outfits would be a conservative estimate), of which 50 of the most memorable went under the hammer at Christie's auction.

It was Catherine who made the greatest contribution to the Princess' transformation from "Shy Sloane" to "Global Do-Gooder." Walker's name is synonymous with Princess Diana, and the fact that the two forged such a close, ongoing relationship for 16 years, speaks volumes. Others fell by the wayside

# Catherine
# WALKER

because they failed to deliver the goods consistently—some were adept at daywear, others at evening dresses, but few had the versatility or ability to dress the Princess around the clock.

Design talent aside, Catherine is a real lady, the soul of discretion and a perfectionist par excellence, qualities the Princess prized. She was always there for the Princess, as indeed Diana was for the designer when she developed breast cancer.

The Princess and the French-woman were similar characters. Both came from broken marriages and they also shared the same shyness.

Ms. Walker studied philosophy at Lille University in France, came to London, met, and married her husband John, who was to die

tragically in an accident, leaving Catherine with two small daughters.

Walker started her career as a dressmaker, initially with children's clothes. Self-taught, she learned the business by trial and error, on-the-job. Despite her inexperience, Catherine succeeded while her peers have fallen from favor. What's more, this is a woman who eschews hype and has never during her 20 years in the business, staged a catwalk show.

Walker's first contribution to the Princess' wardrobe were spotted and faconné jacquard maternity dresses. Hardly a barometer of the shape of things to come, but it was early days. During the course of their brilliant partnership, Walker and Wales liaised on a number of memorable designs,

BELLE DE NUIT ... THE TUDOR TOUCH

*(above)* This show-stopping evening dress was decidedly Elizabethan, with its ruff collar and pointed stomacher-style velvet bodice.

**THE WHITE FANTASTIC** (*above*) The Princess stunned the likes of top American designer Ralph Lauren and *Vogue* editor Anna Wintour in this show-stopping, ice lace sheath at a Washington charity dinner in 1996. It was pure Hollywood.

**PASSAGE TO INDIA** (*top left*) The paste embroidery on the Empire-line bodice of this long dress was evocative of the Mughal style, a compliment to the host country when it was worn on an official visit to India in 1992.

two of them Elizabethan styles; the glittering white beaded dress and jacket named "Elvis" by the press and the Tudor-inspired dress that Diana wore with a huge crucifix to an evening at Garrards the jewelers.

I often marveled at the fact that so many of the POW's outfits for the official overseas tours were so incredibly politically correct, but then one has to remember that Catherine is

after all, an academic, who knows her stuff and studies her subject. She gets engrossed in the technicalities, and will go to embassies to research graphics, embroidery, the precise look and the color of an outfit.

Her client list boasts the likes of the Duchess of Kent and daughter Lady Helen Windsor (whose wedding dress Walker made), Queen Noor of Jordan, and Selina Scott.

To a certain degree, dressing Diana was about power; if designers could control and manipulate the Princess' wardrobe, then that gave them great clout. Catherine, however, was in a different league, being the first person to compliment the Princess if she looked good in another designer's clothes.

Due to her privileged position with the Princess, Walker was the target of a considerable amount of jealousy from her peers, although all admitted that in Catherine Diana had

**SOME ENCHANTED EVENING** (*above left*) This bustle-backed, strapless, pink and blue chintz-print, long evening gown, draped and caught with a bow at the hipline, created a touch of Edwardiana. Worn with an upswept chignon, it danced the night away Down Under in Melbourne at the start of 1988.

**EVERYTHING IS BEAUTIFUL AT THE BALLET** (*above*) For a gala evening at the English National Ballet, of which the Princess was patron, an embroidered, tunic-topped two-piece of shrimp silk. The fabric is used horizontally for the top, and pleated vertically for the long skirt.

found her soul-mate and the designer who was right for her, and they were prepared to credit her accordingly.

At the end of the day, Catherine was a designer for every occasion. She was a chameleon, capable of designing everything from a simple little maternity dress to a full-blown ballgown. And she was always politically correct. Which is why she stayed the course.

# chapter six
# testing times

"I was compelled to go out and do
my engagements and not let people down,
and in a way they supported me."

DIANA, PRINCESS OF WALES

# Mother Courage . . .

**CHECK IT OUT** *(above)* Worn here with a red matador-style hat, Diana's favorite red and white houndstooth check edge-to-edge jacket with black ribbon-slotted trim was a spoof on Chanel-style by witty Italian talent, Franco Moschino.

**VRAI CHANEL** *(below right)* The Gitanes-blue collarless, elongated jacket with contrast braiding, was worn over a matching short pleated skirt with dark leg work on a visit to The British Youth Red Cross in early 1992.

**VIVID VERSACE** *(previous page)* Now that Diana is free to fly any fashion flag she desires, stellar designer Gianni Versace is her new darling. His simple shifts suit her new lifestyle by day, whilst his understated elegance meets with her new minimalistic mood by night. The rich color of this simple long crêpe shift dress, with cutaway shoulderline and notched V-neckline, looked dynamite on Di. A matching clutch bag and multi-strand pearl choker at the neck set it off to perfection for a visit to Chicago in June, 1996.

"I'LL NEVER MARRY unless I really love someone," Diana vowed to her nanny, Mary Clarke, as a child, when her own parents were divorcing. A promise easily made when you are still in the land of make-believe, but we all know what happens to the best-laid plans ...

After the Wedding of the Century, the future looked rosy for the new Princess of Wales, who at the time enthused: "I am absolutely delighted, thrilled, blissfully happy." Which she undoubtedly was at the time.

What a difference a decade makes. As the 90s dawned, it became apparent all was not well with the

## "There were three people in that marriage ..."

DIANA, PRINCESS OF WALES

Waleses, and try as the couple may to put on a united front in public, the word was out. Everyone knew that the "fairy-tale" marriage was falling apart.

Diana's struggle with bulimia, her husband's inability to handle the problem, plus the fact that the Princess would publicly voice: "There were three people in that marriage, so it was rather crowded," were all contributing factors to the breakdown of their union.

Things may not have been working with Charles, but Diana still had her boys. "They mean everything

to me," she would say. "I want my boys to know that Charles did love me when we got married." She also had her work, and her good works. No matter how badly she felt behind locked doors, in public the show had to go on, and Diana was Mother Courage incarnate.

"I was compelled to go out and do my engagements and not let people down, and in a way they supported me," she admitted.

By now the Princess was no fashion fledgling—through the '80s, she had taken a virtual degree course in style, and had passed with honors. She was now into her graduate course.

As every woman knows, a new hairdo can work wonders and lend a girl a whole new lease of life. Which was just what Diana needed.

Enter the super-stylist, flying Scotsman, Sam McKnight, darling of the Supermodel set. He came into Diana's life in 1990, on a *Vogue* shoot, when he was booked to style Diana's hair for some photographs in a tiara.

At the end of the photosession, Diana, who had been duly impressed with Sam's styling, asked the celebrated crimper what he would do with her hair, given carte blanche.

McKnight suggested reducing the volume, and promised that the effect would be to take five years off her.

It was an offer no woman could refuse. Eagerly, Diana gave Sam the go-ahead and free rein to his talents. Out came the scissors, and a more modern, cutting-edge image was created for the Princess, who emerged sleeker and sharper, with a new-found friend for life.

The marriage may have been foundering, but England's Rose continued to bloom, becoming more international in her style. Having paid her dues to British fashion, the Princess no longer felt obliged to confine herself to homegrown labels, and broadened her base. She became ever more international in her style. Yves Saint-Laurent's Rive Gauche, Chanel, Moschino, and Versace all

BELLE IN CHANEL *(above)* The Princess was acquiring quite a wardrobe of Chanels. This one—not so much a suit as a co-ordinated jacket and skirt—features a long-line, wool bouclé, double-breasted jacket with signature Chanel buttons, with contrasting black braid to synchronize with the short, black, pleated skirt, black clutch bag, and pumps. It was worn in Hull, England, in February 1991, for four assignments in one day.

BLACK LOOK *(left)* This magic, yet tragic, black Chanel belted coat-dress quickly became synonymous with sad events in the Princess' life. This same elegant outfit went to the funerals of Diana's father, Lord Spencer, Emperor Hirohito's, and that of her grandmother, Lady Fermoy. A staple standby for such grief-filled occasions.

became familiar designer labels in her wardrobe.

The Princess now shopped around, homing in on the likes of Italian wit, designer Franco Moschino, whose name translates as "little fly." Antiestablishment and irreverent, the fun element appealed to the POW, who would track down his suits at Harvey Nichols. A particular favorite was his striking houndstooth "spoof" Chanel-style suit that Diana ordered with a red and white jacket with a contrasting black and white pencil skirt.

The Princess bought this suit from "Harvey Nicks," which had sold all the skirts at the time and had to order one especially for the Princess. Diana decided to customize her Moschino, requesting the skirt in black and white, rather than in the red and white checkway that matched the jacket. She loved this suit, and it was seen on numerous occasions, initially to meet the boys on a boat and again on a charity mission. It also went to Princess Eugenie's christening.

Says Gai Pearl-Marshall, who represents Moschino in England:

"That picture of the Princess (on the boat) is one of the most lovely moments, visually ... she was so pleased to see the boys."

Another Moschino suit, in forest-green with contrasting black lapels and pocket trim, epaulettes, and brass buttons, with a matching knee-skimming pencil skirt, was an example of her much-loved military mode.

Moschino, who died in September 1994, loved Diana, and dubbed her the "Fairy Princess."

"He was mad about her," recalls Gai Pearl-Marshall, "but, given the choice, he would have preferred to dress the Queen."

Diana had sampled the hors d'oeuvre—her first taste of Chanel was the red coat for her Paris trip. The style appealed, and this initial flirtation proved the start of an *entente cordiale.*

Chanel chic came in the guise of royal blue, too—the black-trimmed jacket partnering a short black skirt. And there was also a black shawl-collared coat-dress, double-breasted and gilt-buttoning, with a wide, boldly gilt buckled, waist-whittling belt. The Princess looked wonderful in this; she

**TWO-TONE CHIC** *(right)* Signature Starzewski style, using his horizontal pleat treatment for a white grosgrain, above-knee skirt, paired with black, cutaway, single-breasted, three-button, fitted jacket with a scoop neckline, and bold buttons. It was worn in June 1991.

**LADY OF SPAIN** *(far right)* Catherine Walker's striking flame-red tunic top is paired with a horizontal satin pleat skirt, punctuated with colored glass buttons. The color corresponds with that used to line the cape of a toreador—perfect for a visit to Expo '92 in Seville, Spain.

**MAN OF THE MOMENT** *(below right)* Tomasz Starzewski's creative talents, and his distinctive horizontal pleating, caught Diana's eye.

always looked magic in black, as most women of that age tend to do. This particular outfit appeared mainly on sad occasions—at the funerals of her father, Lord Spencer, her grandmother, Lady Fermoy, and that of Japanese Emperor, Hirohito, always worn with dramatic, broad-brimmed hats; it also showed up at The Earl of West-moreland's memorial service.

Pop concerts always provided an opportunity for more offbeat dressing, and for a Phil Collins concert in April 1990, Diana chose a midnight-blue velvet pants suit with a double-breasted jacket and con-trasting satin lapels, a twist to her now-familiar tuxedo theme.

As Jacques Azagury has observed, "She was always 'up' on what was happening." Which meant being in touch with the hot new designer names of the day. Two such "happening" labels were Amanda

Wakeley and the Polish-born Tomasz Starzewski.

"I first met Diana at her brother's wedding—10 years ago," remembers Tom. "I found her sweet ... she was sitting at the top of the stairs at Althorp ... it was the day of Lord Spencer's wedding to Victoria Lockwood, actually (Tom designed Victoria's wedding dress). I just thought that she looked very cute, her arms hugging her knees,

**PINK PRINCESS** *(far left)* Diana's pale pink cocktail dress features Tomasz' pleat treatment, interrupted by contrasting black bands, for a visit to a provincial ballet company in 1992.

**SOLID PLUS STRIPES** *(left)* Starzewski's single-breasted, velvet jacket, with lapels and pocket flaps to match the multicolored satin horizontal-pleat skirt, was worn to meet the cast at a Chicken Shed Rock Concert in November 1991.

**MATCHING STYLE** *(below left)* A close-up on those perfect pins, enhanced by the sling-back shoes that Diana herself dubbed "tart's trotters."

**ROUGE ET NOIR** *(below)* One of Diana's best-loved color combinations—a short lacquer-red dress, with contrast-banding in black at the hem and off-the-shoulder neckline, worn to see *Private Lives* in October 1990.

watching the wedding world go by. I didn't see her again until she walked into my Brompton Road shop in 1990. Both Diana and Fergie came in within three months of each other, and both of them had bought the same horizontally-pleated dress of mine from Lucienne Phillips. That dress was a hit—Tania Bryer had it, as did Cosima van Bulow. We made over a thousand of them, and we are still doing this style. In fact, I am just remaking that dress at the moment," he admits.

WIMBLEDON WINNER *(far left)* For her favorite spectator sport, in July 1994—a red silk crêpe-de-chine button-through safari dress with the designer's signature gilt ramshead buttons and belt buckle, by Tomasz Starzewski.

VELVET TOUCHES *(left)* Right from the start, Diana had shown a penchant for velvet trims—here, a sophisticated way with the velvet touch from Tomasz Starzewski—a suit that's not so much a suit, more a coordinating single breasted, long-line jacket in pale pink wool crêpe with chocolate velvet trim to match the pelmet of plain velvet pencil skirt beneath.

outfits a year. I never made any fancy long gowns for her, only suits, dresses, dinner-dresses, and especially tuxedos. She also bought a pale pink wool crêpe jacket with brown velvet pockets and a brown velvet skirt.

"There is a look that the POW had," believes Starzewski. "Tailored, quite conservative. I think she took

conspicuous in those colors. I think that her daywear—and I am partially responsible for that—was probably too serious for someone of that age, and sadly she lost out on not being able to wear the young clothes of her generation. It was a job, and she wore professional, decorative clothes, a working girl's clothes," he comments reflectively.

## "She was always 'up' on what was happening."

JACQUES AZAGURY

"That," concedes Tom, "was the dress that made my career. It was one that worked ... a horizontally-pleated style. Fergie had it in black; Di had pink with two black bands," recalls Tomasz. "Lucienne Phillips sold over 400 of this style."

It goes without question that meeting the Princess changed Tom's career course—"in the sense that we

then consistently made clothes for her up until the last year," he remembers.

"Her first order was an ivory wool crêpe jacket with jeweled buttons and horizontally-pleated skirt. She also had a dress with a drop-waisted blouson, again with horizontal pleats on the skirt, with a boat-shaped neckline. From that point, I dressed her in about six

on board the Royal Family's dress-code, in that she never chose anything sombre, always a color to be noticed, to stand out. She had a particularly English taste in color—you would never see her in those browns and chocolates that American or Italian women love, but then she wouldn't have been

"I believe that her best look was a pair of shorts and a shirt ... she always looked very fresh and very young that way," he observes.

"I made Diana a dinner-suit for Christmas and she wore that. I know that she basically bought from all of us, but she certainly had a budget for me—and a price-limit. Everything

**LEGGY AND LINEAR** *(left)* The epitome of style for the 50th Anniversary of V-J Day in August 1996— a suit in white wool crêpe, with three button, single-breasted jacket with contrasting black tram-lines, echoed by the matching straight skirt by Tomasz Starzewski. Accessories are a high-crowned straw topper and contrast-striped high-heeled shoes, and a single pearl rope at her neck.

we did for her, we did to her measurements, even if it came from a ready-to-wear collection, and it could never exceed £1,800. One of the first things that I made her was a printed dress with ramshead buttons, a cutaway, ankle-length dress that was worn every year in the summer. We never remodelled it, yet it was always worn; probably for five years, consistently," he recalls.

The most striking examples of Tomasz' designs for Diana feature his signature horizontal pleating—the pink and black one; another on similar lines with a black jacket and white skirt; a red cocktail two-piece with circular diamanté buttons on the pleated skirt; and a skirt in multi-bright stripes that were echoed on the suit lapels and pocket trim.

For Wimbledon, in 1994, he made Diana a lacquer-red, sleeveless, safari-pocketed shirt-dress with his trademark ramshead gilt buttons and belt buckle.

Quite the most stunning suit worn by the Princess was his black and white collarless, short-skirted suit that appeared to celebrate the 50th Anniversary of VJ Day, in August 1995.

# Lady in Red

WHETHER IT WAS pure coincidence, or signalling an alert, the Princess did appear to have a penchant for red at this point in her life. The Lady in Red appeared in Derbyshire in June 1990 with Catherine Walker's much-worn scarlet military suit.

Bruce Oldfield's long, V-necked silk chiffon dress in a red and silver-lamé plaid fabric, the bodice draped to mould the body to the hipline, appeared at the premier of *Hot Shots* in 1991; a short, halter-necked, scarlet lace cocktail dress with scalloped hemline by Catherine Walker was sighted on a trip to Argentina; a red-piped, lipstick-pink two-piece (yet another Walker), with an off-the-shoulder, elongated tunic top, was worn at London's Barbican at the start of the new decade; a short, black-banded lacquer-red cocktail dress—a Bruce Oldfield—went to see *Private Lives*; Edelstein's cowl-backed long evening dress was wheeled out for an Italian banquet during that same year; and Catherine Walker's red-hot scarlet suit with tunic top,

banded in satin to synchronize with the short, horizontally-pleated skirt that it partnered, appeared in Seville at Expo '92, to cite but a few well-red examples. A white suit with long-line collarless jacket, that might well have been a Chanel but, it transpired, was yet another Walker, appeared in Japan in 1990, and this, too, was contrast-piped in red.

The year of 1992 marked a watershed in Diana's life. Her relationship with James Hewitt was over. The boys were growing up and less dependent on their mother. Things came to a head in February, during the Waleses passage to India. For all her adulation, her status, her boys, her privileged lifestyle, that famous image of the Princess dressed

**STOLED STYLE** *(far right)* This off the shoulder red and lipstick pink two-piece, with shoulder-slipping jacket over matching pencil skirt, by Catherine Walker, was sighted in November 1990.

**VENETIAN CHIC** *(right)* In the words of its designer, Jacques Azagury, "The red-beaded one that she wore in Venice marked the shortest she's gone to date." The zip-front, tunic-style top skimmed a matching sliver of a skirt.

CLASHING COLOR *(left)* A walk on the bright side in Catherine Walker's tricolored three-piece, comprising a lacquer-red, edge-to-edge jacket, lemon top, and draped, purple, knee-capping skirt. It is accessorized with red and black banded matador hat, and the purple of the boldly self-belted skirt is picked up with matching purple pumps. This outfit was first sighted in Hong Kong, in November 1989, and it appeared, more famously, when Diana was captured in camera alone in front of the imposing Taj Mahal in 1992.

HOT STUFF *(far left)* A sizzling, fiesta-like shade for a Carmen-inspired short, scarlet lace cocktail shaker, with satin rouleau doglead halter-neck, and shoulder-slipping neckline. This proved a perfect choice for dinner on an official visit to Argentina, in November 1995.

in a scarlet (yes, that red, again) bolero jacket—a lone figure seated against the backdrop of the mighty Taj Mahal, the monument to love—said it all. Diana was sending out strong signals, and the message was emphatic: "It's all over now," and "I feel so unloved and alone."

tolerate one another, and there was clearly no hope of a reconciliation. By the end of the year, their separation was made public, in an official announcement by the then Prime Minister, John Major.

This was a relief for Diana, who admitted as the year drew to its close:

## "I simply haven't got anything left to give."

DIANA, PRINCESS OF WALES

The following month was poignant for her, as it saw the death of her beloved father, Lord Spencer.

Charles and Diana's body language on their Korean tour in November of 1992 was telling. Totally ignoring each other, it was blatantly obvious that they could no longer

"I simply haven't got anything left to give." It had been an *annus horribilis*, as the Queen might have put it.

At last the Prisoner of Wales could look forward to her release. In the meantime, the official separation meant the rules and regulations of The Firm could be somewhat more relaxed, as Diana was in a halfway House of Windsor situation. Her dress began to reflect this new-found freedom. Her legs, one of the best pairs in the business, started getting more of a look-in, with leg-revealing slits and splits.

Like the long eau-de-nil and cream silk crêpe sheath, with an off-the-shoulder neckline and striped bodice, slit to the knee, by Catherine Walker, that Diana wore to the premier of *Accidental Hero* in April 1993. A Bellville-Sassoon variation on the theme was Lorcan Mullany's slinky long black slip-dress worn to *Romeo & Juliet* two months later.

During 1993, the Princess' hemlines, too, became visibly briefer than ever before—partly a fashion barometer, partly indicative of Diana's freer spirit.

Despite the separation, or perhaps because of it, the Princess' workload continued relentlessly as she tried to lose herself in her public duties.

Her work overload and the stress of the impending divorce, coupled with fears of palace conspiracies, finally got the better of her. She veered towards black clothes, perhaps a symbol of "mourning for her lost life," but in so doing, she managed to eclipse Diana the clotheshorse in favor of Diana the workhorse.

A war was also being waged between the Waleses—a struggle for supremacy, for centerstage, and for the boys. Distressed at the appointment of Tiggy Legge-Bourke as their minder, distraught at the constant posse of paparazzi trailing her every move, Diana decided to

**BEST DRESSED GUEST** *(above)* For the marriage of Lady Sarah Armstrong-Jones to Daniel Chatto, in July 1994, Diana wore Walker's tailored, black, satinized wool dress, with white collar and cuffs, set off with a broad-brimmed hat.

**MINT CONDITION** *(right)* The shoulder-baring and leg-revealing trademarks were both encapsulated in CW's slit-skirted dinner dress.

withdraw from public life, for the time-being at least.

The Princess chose to make her farewell announcement at a charity luncheon at London's Hilton Hotel in December 1993, at which she was guest of honor.

For the occasion, she wore a stylish green suit with her trademark contrast velvet touches, designed by rising British star, Amanda Wakeley. The designer—a blonde, British beauty of a similar age to Diana—first

"There were no airs and graces; she was just incredibly friendly, relaxed and open. I was admiring her tan and said 'Oh how well you look', and she said: 'Oh, I am so naughty—I've been on those sunbeds again.'"

The first outfit that the Princess had from Wakeley was a navy-blue crêpe, double-breasted pants-suit with a pearl tassel.

"Diana had a lot of stunning suits and what I call 'luxury weekend wear'—like skinny pants, cashmere bodies, and sweaters," says Amanda. "The ironic thing with her choice of my clothes is that we are known for glamorous evening wear, which was her signature. I was surprised that she never really came to me for her evening wear. I think that she dressed for people's expectations of her, whereas I am certain that she would have worn some of our evening wear to private functions.

"She had the most beautiful body. She didn't need the bells and whistles—she had wonderful arms, great shoulders, a great bosom, and good skin. I know because I used to go to the same gym as her, and she worked very hard at it."

The year 1993 saw the start of a more modern, glamorous phase that was to reach its zenith in the months before Diana's tragic death.

Two years earlier, the POW had bought a wicked little black dress—the only model she would ever buy from Christina Stambolian. She had kept this dress in her wardrobe, saving it for the right moment.

That occasion was a fund-raising dinner at London's Serpentine Gallery, of which the Princess was patron. Coincidentally, this was the very same evening in June that Prince Charles had chosen to confess his adultery in an interview with Jonathan Dimbleby on prime time TV. Thirteen million viewers watched the Prince's show, but Diana did it her way and went out to play. The famous dress that came to be dubbed the "Divorce" dress marked a turning point.

She certainly stole Charles' thunder. But then, didn't she always? She may have been a Princess in the wilderness during the first few months of her separation, but now she was a cat on a hot tin roof.

met the POW in 1992, at her first premises in London's Ifield Road.

Amanda remembers their first meeting: "I think that her secretary rang up and made an appointment for her. Diana arrived early—I'll never forget opening the door to her. She was like an apologetic schoolgirl standing there on one leg, with the other tucked behind her. Her face looked young and she looked at me with that really coy expression that she had. She was just charming, and so relaxed and low-key.

IT TOOK A SCORPIO (purportedly the sexiest sign of the zodiac) to create this "wicked" little black bomb-shell of a "statement" dress. And if that's what it took, it was worth every penny of the $1,500 that it cost the Princess, and more. You just couldn't put a price on the impact it created. With hindsight, this little number would become the most famous of all the Princess' dresses. It was, in its way, the '90s equivalent of the celebrated Emanuel "Engagement" dress, and it came to be dubbed the "Divorce" dress. But before we go any further, let's put the record straight—this sexy LBD (Little Black Dress) was not, repeat not, designed by Valentino, as claimed by many at the time. Nor was it the "Little Black

# Christina
# STAMBOLIAN

Off-The-Peg Dress" as it has often been wrongly dubbed. So whodunit?

It was, in fact, the work of Christina Stambolian, a one-off, one-and-only, special, made-to-measure dress for the Princess. And Diana wore it on a day that marked a turning-point in her life.

Stambolian may only ever have made this one dress for the Princess, but it was dynamite by virtue of both its style and its association. Nice one, Di, and one in the eye for Charlie boy. This was the dress Diana donned the night of Prince Charles' interview with Jonathan Dimbleby, when he affirmed his adultery with Camilla Parker Bowles. So it was seminal. Hell hath no fury, and all that.

The Princess had kept this dress in her wardrobe for quite a while, and was obviously waiting for the right moment to wear it. That evening could not have been more opportune. The objective was to knock her husband off the front pages. And it worked. It was not only a Statement dress, but a Result dress.

And all we fashion editors got egg on our faces. Italian designer Valentino had issued a press release stating that the Princess would be wearing his dress for that memorable evening. But he got it wrong, underestimating Diana, who changed her mind at the last minute and decided not to opt for the Val number, after all.

**WATCH THESE SWATCHES** (above) Black silk jacquard and chiffon—the potent recipe for the little black dress that Stambolian sketched (right).

Naturally, we all took The Chic's (as he is dubbed) press release as gospel and had to eat humble pie, apologize to Ms. Stambolian, and put the record straight in our publications.

Which is how I came to meet the vivacious Greek designer lady in the first place. Christina Stambolian hails from Volos, and studied fashion, art and theater costume for four years at Vacalao Art College, in Athens.

Christina arrived in London in 1970. Four years later she started working with Harold Horwitz, who backed her, financing her own-name store in London's Beauchamp Place, the POW's favorite stamping ground, a few doors down from Di's favorite Italian eaterie, San Lorenzo.

Although the celebrated "Statement" dress was bought at the end of the summer of 1991, it was not until the end of June, three years later that we got to see it. Perhaps Diana was waiting for an opportune moment. A flashback to 1991, then:

"The Princess just walked into my shop—I had bumped into her before in the 'ladies' at San Lorenzo—Diana walked in together with her brother Lord Spencer. I couldn't believe it at the time; she was a crazy girl, really fun," recalls Stambolian.

The Princess had never actually met Christina before, although she had bought one of the designer's bicolored red and black wool dresses and a couple of ready-to-wear blouses, as Christina remembers.

"When she came to my shop with her brother," recalls Christina, "Diana told me that she wanted a dress designed for a special occasion,

although she didn't elaborate, so we started talking and I showed her things—I drew a few ideas for her."

"I decided on something quite open and bare. The Princess started laughing—'No way will I have anything too open or my arms showing,' she said, but I managed to convince her. In the end she asked her brother for his opinion ... he just left it up to her. At the time she was against black, and the two were considering an ivory color, which Diana thought too virginal. Finally she agreed to black, and we went for it—a short black dress with V-bodice in silk jacquard, falling onto a chiffon skirt using Italian fabrics from my supplier in Como.

"The Princess asked us to ring her when it was ready, but refused to make an appointment. She just popped in one day, unannounced, for her fitting, and my Giovanna took her measurements. Then everything was sent to the Palace, with someone from the shop," remembers the designer.

"It was a change in keeping with her new life. At the time she came to me, I thought that, as everyone was 'dressing' her, I'd opt for something that was 'less dressed and more Diana'. It took her some time to get around to wearing it—in June 1994. I suppose that she must have found it too bare and daring at the time," comments Stambolian.

**DIANA THE DIVA** *(right)* Prince Charles might have been doing his Dimbleby interview, but you can't keep a good woman down or, for that matter, off the front pages. In her daring dress, this would prove to be Diana's finest hour.

# chapter seven
# new-found style

"The last dresses that I made
for her were very sexy."

JACQUES AZAGURY

# Let's get physical

**A LITTLE WHITE DRESS** *(above)* Epitomizing the Princess' new pared-down style statement— Versace's short, simple, ivory shift dress with a collarless neckline filled in with single pearl choker.

**NIGHT SHIFT** *(below right)* An Italian label was "de rigeur" for Luciano's concert in Modena, Italy, in September 1995. Out came this sensuous, body-molding, little white dress, with Versace's signature Medusa-head trim on the straps.

**ARRIVIDERCI VERSACE** *(below far right)* In July 1997, the Princess was in Milan for the memorial service of her friend, who once called her "the Mother Teresa and Cindy Crawford of our time." She wears his shift-dress and leather Kelly bag with Medusa heads, re-named "the Diana bag."

**SEXY LITTLE NUMBER** *(previous page)* Diana bought this strappy, sensuous little black silk crêpe shift dress from Versace's shop, and wore it to the premier of *Apollo 13* in 1995.

A SINGLE, POWERFUL stride in a wicked little black number from a little Greek lady in Beauchamp Place said it all. A giant step forward for womankind. The Princess blazed a trail for what was to follow—a new-found style and sophistication marked the shape of things to come. Call it the "Divorce" or "Statement" dress, this is the significant bit of little black magic that started the ball rolling. "I'll show them that I'm made of stronger stuff," Diana seemed to be saying.

Even during the interim between the separation and the divorce, a new body awareness and body language became manifest in the Princess' dress code. Her clothes were en route to becoming a class act, a parade of international style.

Diana began to accentuate the positive. She revealed a new awareness of bareness; took a pride in her body beautiful. Those once skeletal shoulders and bony back were eclipsed by a well-worked-out torso. Sleeveless little shift-dresses now revealed firm, healthy arms. Necklines plunged to new lows, revealing maximum exposure with cleavage and décolletage. Strappy, sexy high-heeled shoes and seductive sandals from the *crème-de-la-crème* of shoemakers—Blahnik and Choo, and Gina—complemented hemlines being worn at an all-time-high, and lent the Princess an even longer, leaner line of leg.

There is no denying that Diana was now in sublime shape, and she flaunted it in an easy, understated style, embracing fashion's new minimalist mood. Simple, easy shapes, such as short, sleeveless shift dresses by Italian designer Gianni Versace, occasionally from his "Atelier" couture label, and Catherine Walker, become staples of her daytime wardrobe,

## "The Mother Teresa and Cindy Crawford of our time."

GIANNI VERSACE

appearing in ivory, scarlet, lilac, and black. These styles are not unlike those worn by fashion icon Jacqueline Kennedy-Onassis in her heyday.

Halter necks enhance that superb shoulderline, and daring décolletage defines her bust. Short, dress-makery

suits, with curvy little nipped-in jackets paired with flirty, well-above-the-knee skirts, become the norm, and those high-voltage bright colors are, for the most part, exchanged for a palette of powdered pales—cooler pastels such as blues, pistachios, and soft sugar-pinks.

Off-duty, too, Diana affects an international style—a throwaway chic, very BCBG (*Bon Chic, Bon Genre*); the Gallo-Italo put-together of navy blazer, white jeans, and T-shirt; or a long-line, fitted pinstripe suit. The same suit jacket is recycled over blue

VOGUE

JULY
£2.70

**Happy Birthday**

THE PRINCESS
OF WALES
New portraits

9 770262 213036    07>

**BIRTHDAY GIRL** *(left)* July 1994 marked Diana's 33rd birthday, and to celebrate the occasion, the man with the golden lens, Patrick Demarchelier, took this relaxed, smiling picture of her for *Vogue*. She is wearing a navy blue, halter-necked, silk crêpe short dress by Catherine Walker. Sam McKnight took care of her hair, and her make-up was by Mary-Jane Frost.

**WHITE NIGHT** *(above)* Borrowed for the occasion, and now stored in a bank vault, this long, white lace Catherine Walker evening dress, with cutaway, haltered shoulderline, proved a stunner at a charity benefit in aid of breast cancer in September 1996.

**SCOOP** *(overleaf)* To receive her well-deserved Humanitarian Award at New York's Hilton Hotel, in December 1995, the Princess wore a humdinger of a dress, with daring décolletage—the "wicked" Versace cross-back number that made its début on the night of her "Panorama" screening.

**BABY BLUE** *(above)* The Princess had a penchant for pretty pastelry at this time, a predilection for baby and sugar blues and pinks. Pictured here at Cook County Hospital, in Chicago, in June 1996, she wears Versace's summerweight, wool, tailored suit jacket, with silver edged covered buttons, and a matching short pencil skirt. Accessories, too, are by Versace, the shoes being part of a batch made especially for Diana.

**IN THE PINK ... THE PASTEL PRINCESS** *(left)* England's Rose is positively blooming in a blush pink, soft wool worsted spring suit. The hip-skimming jacket, with three-quarter length bracelet sleeves, and matching short pencil skirt are by Catherine Walker. Seen leaving London's Savoy Hotel for the *Daily Star* Gold Awards in March 1997, the more sharply shaped, straighter, slightly longer hairstyle makes the Princess look both younger and more "of the moment."

**TRAVELING LIGHT** *(above)* Campus chic—laid back, low-key, could be anybody really, but it just happens to be off-duty Di, in uniform Euro-chic put together with a piece from the other side of the pond. Caught at the airport, en route for a short break in Spain in May 1996, the Princess wears a baseball cap, brass-buttoning classic navy blazer, and blue jeans—every inch the contemporary young traveler.

**DOWN TO EARTH** *(right)* Workaday wear for the Princess of the People, and a newly cultivated antifashion look—simple white shirt, stone-washed blue jeans, and shades worn headband style—epitomizes a new cool chic.

**WORKOUT WEAR** *(far left)* For another visit to Chelsea Harbour Club in November 1995, all a girl needs is a graffiti'd sweatshirt, cycling shorts, uniform trainers, and those indispensable "shades."

**DRESSING DOWN** *(left)* A long, scarlet double-breasted coat with black buttons and leg-revealing deep back vent is thrown over her workout gear, but the do-it-yourself hairdo, white sox, and trainers are a giveaway.

**BAD HAIR DI?** *(below left)* Back to basics—a very sportif put-together for the royal school run: navy single-breasted pinstripe blazer, worn over white T-shirt; white tracksuit pants tucked into tan Western boots; and hair concealed under a casual baseball cap.

**WHERE EAGLES DARE** *(below)* A very American look, with emblazoned baseball jacket, is perfect for taking the boys back to school.

Separation saw Diana at her best and most provocative. She socked it to us with a posse of short, sharp outfits, each one sexier than the last. Her zest for life was reflected with a fizzy, orange bouclé, short-skirted suit with curvy, fitted, short jacket and neat, Peter Pan collar, by Gianni Versace. Cinched with an ultra-narrow black belt, this was worn over a classic black a long, black dress, with a corded-lace bodice, falling onto a silk georgette and crêpe-de-chine skirt with fishtail train. All her familiar feminine wiles were brought into play on that particular evening—the cross-back straps lending an exciting exit-line, and the daringly deep décolletage was redolent of that first careless (albeit innocent) rapture with the

## "Lady Di inspired Lady Dior."

BERNARD DANILLON DE CAZELLA

polo neck to brighten up the day for the patients at Liverpool Women's Hospital, in November.

Diana's "Panorama" interview took place in November of 1995. Rather than sit at home biting her nails and reproaching herself for what might have been, she went out and about to celebrate. Socialite Anoushka Hempel threw a screening party to celebrate the occasion, and Diana was a veritable bombshell in

Emanuels black taffeta long evening dress, a.k.a. the "Engagement" dress. It was as though the Princess had travelled full circle—the Emanuel dress marked her first rustle of spring, being in taffeta, full-skirted and girly, with a ruffled décolletage, while the "Panorama" one, designed by Jacques Azagury, was sleek, sexy, and sophisticated. One marked the beginning of the story; the other, the end—well almost.

**ELEGANT IN BLACK** *(left)* The Princess was something of a "bag-lady" in fashion speak. Here, a handbag accompanies an elegant suit by Valentino as Diana meets Mme Chirac on the steps of the Elysée Palace in October 1995.

**SIMPLY RED** *(far left)* A scarlet silk, satin-bodiced, décolleté shift dress with bowed bustline detail is worn with matching bag and shoes. By Paris designer, Christian Lacroix, this was a fitting choice for an evening at the capital's Petit Palais.

**BAGS OF STYLE** *(below left)* The first prototype of what was to become known as the "Lady Dior," given to her while she was in Paris, proved very popular with the Princess.

Diana's association with the bag did it no harm at all! As Dior's Bernard Danillon de Cazella says: "Of course it helped the sales of the bag. The whole story started with the picture of the Princess carrying the bag. She loved it, because she bought a few more at the Dior store in London. Lady Di inspired Lady Dior."

Despite all the trauma on the run-up to the divorce announcement, in February 1996, Diana continues to shine. Her image becomes even more high-profile. Style-wise, she is stream-lined, on a roll, well on the way to becoming her own woman again.

In August 1996, the Wales' divorce becomes absolute, and for "Divorce" day the Princess wears Ronit Zilkha's pale blue suit with contrast cream-braided shawl collar.

Diana now has to pick up the threads of her life and start over. She is about to re-invent herself in perhaps her truest form for what is to prove the last chapter in her life.

One particular handbag style—which came to be dubbed the "Lady Dior" after Diana—is becoming ever-present on the Princess' person. It is like a uniform, indispensable, appearing here, there, and everywhere. Double-handled, in quilted black leather, with gilt ringed eyelets, it sports several gilt taglike charms hanging from the handle. Back at the *Daily Express*, I am asked to track down said handbag to ascertain whether we can obtain one for a reader competition. This proved a mission impossible at the time. Now all has been revealed.

The bag, it transpired, hailed from Christian Dior, and thereby hangs a tale. Bernard Arnault, Chairman of LVMH, who heads up Louis Vuitton, Moët Chandon, Dior, Lacroix, Kenzo, *et al.*, had been courting Diana as an international woman of substance. He had invited the Princess to Paris for the Cézanne retrospective at Le Grand Palais, when Diana was given a present of what was to become Dior's best-selling bag, by the President's wife, Bernadette Chirac. It was the first prototype of a new leather model, made expressly for the occasion, and when we first saw it, it was a one-off, as yet unavailable in the stores.

THE CASABLANCA KID Jacques Azagury was probably the last designer to see Diana. "It was two weeks before she went on her trip; the morning that she left for Greece with Rosa Monckton," he remembers.

Azagury made some 18 dresses for Diana, the most memorable being the galactic, velvet-bodiced dance dress that made its debut in Florence in 1985, and reappeared in Toronto the following year.

Other notable Azagury numbers were "the red, beaded one she wore in Venice, which marked the shortest she'd gone to date; the "Panorama" one that she also wore in New York with Kissinger admiring her cleavage, and the black one that she wore on her 36th birthday," recalls Azagury.

"She was such a darling to deal with. Sometimes she'd come in out of the blue—'Carry on with the other customers, I can wait,' she'd say. That was the kind of person that she was. Just so charming and really, really funny, with this really great sense of humor, who quite liked to lark about."

# Jacques
# AZAGURY

**MEMORIES ARE MADE OF THIS** (above)

A framed montage takes pride of place on the wall of Jacques Azagury's shop. Illustrating three of the dresses that he made for Diana (the long, red, beaded dress with slashed-across neckline, the blue one seen at top right, and her 36th birthday present, seen in its full glory opposite), it was her very individual way of saying "Thank you."

"There was a certain time where the clothes that she wore were not really my kind of clothes. I have never done big ballgowns or frilly fashions. Mine is a more sexy, slimmer silhouette than the typical English Rose dresses that she adopted for a certain period in her life," he explains.

"She always made the effort to look good for her public, but over her last 18 months to two years we saw a total change in her wardrobe and 'up' became the operative word. Her clothes were upbeat—sharp, short, tight, obviously because she was feeling so right in herself, and felt that she could carry those dresses."

"And she was always her own person. On the night of her 36th birthday, at the Tate Gallery centenary dinner, Chanel, who were sponsoring the evening, wanted her to wear their dress, but she wore one of mine instead," he emphasizes, proudly.

"The last dresses that I made for her were very sexy, but it has to be said that the whole fashion mood was sexy; there was a lot of cleavage, and slinky, figure-hugging clothes, so it was a reflection of a fashion 'happening' rather than her saying 'I am going to flaunt it'. Don't forget that this was a completely different woman we're talking about," the designer explains.

There was, however, one stunning Azagury dress, the one that got away,

**VERY BLUE** (above) Jacques' sky-blue, pleated silk embroidered georgette, square-necked, short cocktail dress, with daring décolletage and bow-trimmed shoulder straps, was worn to the ballet *Swan Lake* in June 1997.

a black number that tragically, Diana never lived to wear and enjoy.

"It was black, about the most daring dress that she would ever have worn, with a very, very deep plunge back, beaded with a long train. She was going to wear it to the premier of *Hercules* in October 1997. We had done the last fitting the day before she went away, and she loved it," he enthuses.

Taking pride of place in Azagury's Knightsbridge shop is a framed montage. "Dearest Jacques ... lots of love from Diana," it reads. It shows the POW, photographed in the last dresses the designer made for her.

Jacques recalls the day Diana died: "That Sunday, I came in and cleared the shop windows, just placed her picture on the black velvet chair in the window. We then put a couple of red roses on the chair each day, and on the Thursday, my father picked up one of the roses—the water had taken on the shape of a heart droplet, leaving the imprint of a perfect heart-shape," says Jacques sadly.

"Even more bizarre was that, between 11 and midday that day, we were going through the rails and a big moth just flew out. Now, in the Muslim religion, the moth is symbolic of the soul and spirit of the person. The heart droplet represented Diana, and the moth was Dodi."

That was the last goodbye.

**BELLE DE NUIT** *(right and far right)* For the Tate Gallery's Chanel-sponsored centenary gala dinner, on her 36th birthday, Diana chose Azagury's long black, beaded, Chantilly lace dress—and she looked a million dollars. Jacques' sketch *(above)* shows the front, and cross-back straps, of the famous "Panorama"/Humanitarian Awards dress.

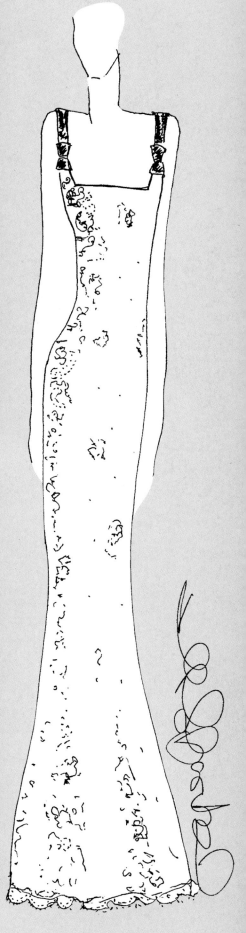

# chapter eight

# the real diana

"The biggest transformation
took place once the Princess
got divorced."

DAVID SASSOON

# The Younger Stateswoman

**A NEW SIMPLICITY** *(above)* "That night she looked stunning, wearing a long, royal blue, body-hugging sheath with straps crossed at the back, like a bathing suit, from her favorite designer Catherine Walker ... it was such a sexy, unprincessy look," comments *Harper's Bazaar* editor, Liz Tilberis, of Diana's CFDA awards outfit, in her autobiography *No Time To Die*.

**WHITE AND WONDERFUL** *(previous page)* Perfect for a midsummer day, Diana wore this slub-silk Catherine Walker dress, with gilt buttons and belt buckle, for a visit to a Hindu Mission in Neasden, North London, in June 1997. The pearl/gilt Chanel earrings echo the white/gold theme.

DAVID SASSOON OBSERVES: "The biggest transformation took place once the Princess got divorced—then she no longer had to wear British designs, so she spread her wings, and opened the wardrobe to Versace, Valentino, and Dior; her image became more starry; her skirts shorter, her necklines lower and more décolleté; her shapes curvier.

"She was aware of the importance of the body shape; she had worked on it and learned to bring out the best in herself; she was happy, having come to terms with who she was—an independent lady who did her own thing. The last year of her life was the real Diana let loose, and my goodness, did she fly!" remarks Sassoon.

Little did we know then that the Princess' time on this earth was to be so cruelly short, and that very soon England's Rose would disappear from our lives forever.

The last year of Diana's life was certainly action-packed. It was a year, almost to the day, with a diary that spanned from one "D" Day (Divorce) on August 28, 1996—the date that her divorce became absolute—to the "D" Day that marked the tragic end of her life in the city of love, Paris, on August 31, 1997.

Now a one-woman show, Diana became increasingly more courageous and confident. She was putting on a brave front in every sense of the word.

The Princess would reveal two complementary aspects of her persona—the understated elegance of the international woman, and the sharing, caring humanitarian—a combination of fashion and compassion that meant both dressing-up and dressing-down. It may seem frivolous to mention fashion and compassion in the same breath, but the fact is, had the Princess not been blessed with a wealth of physical attributes, she might never have become such a superstar on the international stage. Somehow the two worked in tandem.

Diana may no longer be the wife of the future king, but she is still the future king's mother. Meanwhile she's doing her own thing and doing it beautifully. She's still keeping up appearances and good works, too. Sweet charity is what she is all about. The month after her divorce, Diana appears looking dynamite in white—a long, slinky lace sheath with cutaway shoulder-line by Catherine Walker—for a gala dinner in aid of breast cancer in Washington. She also looks the business in a softly-tailored trouser suit for a meeting with Hilary Clinton, America's First Lady.

That same month, Diana flies to Rimini, Italy, to collect an award for her humanitarian work. The Princess wears Ronit Zilkha's royal blue suit with gilt buttons.

For the reception afterward, as a salute to her hosts, she wears a short, black sleeveless shift with cut-away shoulder line by Gianni Versace, set off with a simple, single-strand pearl choker at the neck.

Another spectacular Versace number, this time a long turquoise satin one-shouldered column dress, appeared at the Sydney Entertainment Centre for a dinner in aid of the Victor Chang Cardiac Research. The following month, December, marked the joint début of

> "She was happy, having come to terms with who she was."
>
> DAVID SASSOON

Diana and Galliano, with the first sighting of a dress made in the Dior couture workroom. It was the designer's controversial long lace-embellished slip-style evening dress worn by the Princess for the Costume Institute in New York. A little naughty, a little nightie-like. Diana was fast becoming mistress of her own wardrobe, rather than a wardrobe-mistress.

A flashback to July of 1996 sees Diana's eldest son, Prince William, come up with a gem of an idea—the

**LA BELLA DIANA** *(above and left)* Diana in Italy, at a reception at The Grand in Rimini, to celebrate her well-deserved gold medal for humanitarian services, for which occasion a little signature shift by Versace and a four-strand pearl choker proved appropriate.

**SHE LOOKED THE BUSINESS** *(far left)* Pinstriped Princess dressed in practical, double-breasted pantsuit, epitomizing the uniform that the woman of the '90s wears in the workplace the world over. Here, Diana is en route to meet Hilary Clinton, in September 1996.

suggestion that his mother auction for charity some of those couture dresses she no longer wears. Since her resignation from public life, the Princess has pared down both her wardrobe and her once burdensome workload, editing the latter down to a clutch of those causes that are dearest to her heart.

Over a lunch with Christie's chairman, Christopher Balfour, the Princess outlines the plan; Balfour in turn assigns this special project to Christie's creative director, Meredith Etherington-Smith.

Etherington-Smith comes up with a marvellous motto for the Princess' Sale—"Sequins Save Lives."

Diana was totally "cool" about putting many of her "yesterdays" under the hammer for a good cause— her pet charities. She also thought it would be fun to become involved in the project from start to finish, and expressed this interest.

"Won't you be sorry to see them go?" Meredith asked Diana at their first meeting. "No, I really won't— there are far too many I will never wear again, so why shouldn't I do something useful with them? William

**VIRTUOSO VERSACE** *(right)* Epitomizing the New Diana and her minimalist mode, albeit by night—a simple, toga-style, long sheath dress with notched neckline in vibrant turquoise silk worn with a matching clutch bag to a party in Sydney in 1996.

had such a clever idea, don't you think?" Diana replied.

What the world needed now, as did Diana, was love, sweet love, and the Princess was ready to give all she could with open arms.

Poised and polished, Diana is ready to take on the world—and she will. The Princess is in great shape physically. She has exercised; now she will exorcise all those ghosts from her past. She will throw herself into the role she loves—the humanitarian work that is second nature to her.

The Christie's auction of the dresses from her past was to be her catharsis, so it was with renewed energy that Diana began the new year.

She reached her zenith in this final year. Hitherto, as Amanda Wakeley so succinctly puts it, "Diana had sacrificed her own personal taste to please her public; she did what was expected of her before she did what she wanted to do. At the end, I think that the two really came together.

"To me, she was looking the best she had ever looked towards the end. She was getting her style right—the hair and makeup, so pared down, getting rid of the perms—and she was at ease within her own body, which is when a woman becomes truly beautiful. It is that whole thing about beauty from within. She was happy

**THINKING PINK** (*above*) A bouclé wool tailored suit with longish fitted jacket and abbreviated pencil skirt, by Gianni Versace, is caught in camera following a lunch at Diana's favorite eaterie, San Lorenzo, in London's Beauchamp Place.

**SHORT SHIFT** (*left*) We saw a posse of signature shift dresses emerge from her wardrobe during the final year of Diana's life. They were usually by Versace or Catherine Walker. This one, in red silk, is Walker's, conspicuous on account of the reverse gilt "C"s on the fabric belt.

with her public persona and what she was wearing to events and appearances, and she was really getting it right. If the truth be known, she didn't actually have an image of personal style, like perhaps Jackie 'O'. That comes very easily and naturally to some women, but the Princess really had to work at it," she comments.

Which she certainly did. Diana reinvented herself yet again, and this time she was, as the French say, "*bien dans sa peau*," happy within herself and with herself.

She began to take on the stature and allure of an icon such as Jackie Onassis or Audrey Hepburn, to dress in the same calculated, yet "throwaway," way and enjoy fashion for fashion's sake. As Christina Stambolian so rightly observed: "Recently, she looked more modern."

She had managed to shrug off her royal responsibilities. Having learned a helluva' lot on her journey, Diana could now carve out a niche for herself, and she was happy to throw herself into her own crusades.

"Anywhere that I see suffering is where I want to be, doing what I can," she said. Such as in war-torn Angola and Bosnia, both places that she would visit during 1997.

She began 1997 with a Red Cross visit to Angola in January. This is the off-the-peg Princess of the People, who, appropriately, confines her working wardrobe to functional, practical chameleonic clothes—cool, classic pieces such as blue jeans paired with a sleeveless chambray shirt, worn with navy Superga

sneakers that cost $65 from Russell & Bromley, or lopped-off Chinos with Tod's loafers, a uniform more redolent of her former sister-in-law, Princess Anne, in a similar, albeit slightly more cutting-edge, situation.

The classic Euro-chic navy blazer, jeans, chambray shirt, and Supergas are about the most formal she gets.

"Her last few months were devoted to causes. I think that she enjoyed the dressing-up thing, but people kept commenting on what she was wearing, rather than the charity, and she didn't like to be seen as a clothes-horse. It was when she wore plain shirts and pants that she really shone out," says Liz Emanuel.

The Princess was a great leveler. She could be both saint and super-model. On the one hand, Diana could be on equal terms with Mother Teresa; on the other, with catwalk queen Linda Evangelista.

Designer Zandra Rhodes reflects on Diana's openness and accessibility:

**SAD DAY** *(above)* Celebrated photographer Terence Donovan had often photographed Diana. Here she is pictured leaving his memorial service, together with his wife, another Diana. Princess Di marks her respects in a black-velvet-trimmed jacket over a shift dress by Catherine Walker.

**RIGHT FOR A FIRST NIGHT** *(left)* Long midnight-blue décolleté lace fabric for a scoop-necked, cleavagey dress by Catherine Walker, worn to the premier of *Love and War*.

## "It was when she wore plain shirts and pants that she really shone out."

LIZ EMANUEL

"We were first introduced at the Royal Academy when she was with Prince Charles, who did a double-take at my pink punk hair.

"Later, she came round to my shop with Fergie; the two of them just bounced in like two young girls. I believe that she had possibly wanted to meet me before but, possibly because of my hair, I think that I was considered quite outrageous at the time," Zandra chuckles.

"It is through the Americans that she became known to people of our age. The Americans haven't got royalty, so they think that you can just

**CONTEMPORARY CLASSICS** *(left)* The ubiquitous uniform of the seasoned globe-trotter—basic double-breasted, brass-buttoning blazer, worn over a simple shirt, with blue-jeans and tennis shoes, not forgetting the "must-have" cosmopolitan "shades."

**FASHION WITH A PURPOSE** *(far left)* Charitable chic saw a new, detuned Diana in plain white chambray shirt, belted over khaki-beige Capri pants worn on a Red Cross visit to Angola in January 1997.

**PRACTICAL SNEAKERS** *(below)* The essential foot-finish for the *cognoscenti*—canvas Supergas, made in Italy and available in every conceivable shade. Di's classic navy and white ones hailed from favorite cobblers Russell & Bromley, in London's Bond Street.

go up to them and talk to them and meet them like ordinary human beings. It is only when she became 'lionized', and America took her on, that everyone came to talk about her as if she was one of us; it isn't something that we would even have considered doing over here," believes Zandra.

Back in London, in February, the Princess looks suitably glamorous for the premier of *Love and War*, in a long navy evening dress of Riechers lace with décolleté front; a volte-face reveals the exit line—a sensuous sheer floral lace insert, one of her favorite ploys, designed by Catherine Walker.

And Diana was a great Chanel aficionado, too; she really loved Karl Lagerfeld's suits and accessories, and she owned a number of handbags and

**COLOR IT NEW, COLOR IT BLUE** *(top)*
White flecked cotton tweed for a single-breasted
spring suit from Chanel worn with Jackie
Kennedy style pillbox, as the Princess and
her younger son attend Prince William's
Confirmation Service at Windsor, in the early
spring of 1997.

**POSITIVELY BLOOMING** *(right)* This same
pastel-blue and white Chanel suit received yet
another airing the following month when the
Princess had an English rose, a flower that she
epitomized, named after her. This time the suit
was worn more casually, without a hat.

**DIANA SINGS THE BLUES** "During the last year she went very blue—because of her eyes and blonde hair, she looked good in any of the blue spectrum, right from the pale blues, through to purple," comments Jacques Azagury. And how right he was, as these outfits by Catherine Walker *(left)*, Gianni Versace *(top)*, and Ronit Zilkha *(above)* so eloquently prove.

pairs of shoes. Sometimes she'd come into the store; on other occasions, things would be sent on approval direct to Kensington Palace.

The year of 1997 was a sad one, as it would mark the passing of the Princess, as well as designer Gianni Versace and Mother Theresa, both close friends of Diana's. It also saw the memorial service for leading fashion photographer, Terence Donovan, who had died at the end of 1996. Diana was a good friend of both Terry and his wife, Diana, and in March 1997 the Princess attended the final farewell to this talented lensman.

For the service, she looked both elegant and correct in a chic black shift dress and long-line jacket, featuring her signature velvet touches, gilt clasp closure by Catherine Walker, and accessorized with that indispensable Lady Dior bag.

During the last year of her life, the Princess was still into pretty, pastelly shades—baby blue hues, pistachios, and soft pinks—stylish sophistication translated into a feminine palette.

A Chanel suit in powder-blue cotton tweed flecked with white had appeared at Prince William's confirmation service at Guard's Chapel, Windsor, in February. It was worn with a matching pillbox hat, and the whole outfit was very much in the style of Jackie 'O'.

The Princess took a shine to this particular suit, and it was wheeled out again, this time worn hatless, for a British Lung Foundation charity, when Diana had an English rose named after her.

She had a penchant for blue at this particular time—there was a Versace, a Ronit Zilkha, and a Catherine Walker, all slightly different variations on the theme, in varying tones of pastel blue.

As the weather warmed up, the Princess exchanged those pastel baby-blue suits for stylish sleeveless shift dresses, but a visit to the Centrepoint Charity, for a cold weather project, called for Diana to wear a classic navy-blue blazer paired with gray flannel pants—extremely simple, but Euro-chic yet again.

A stunning double-breasted Prince of Wales checked suit with long-line jacket, from Galliano's début collection for the House of Dior in January, selected by the Princess from the show video, was first sighted in May, when Diana revisited the intensive-care unit of St Mary's Hospital, London, where her two sons were born. This visit by the Princess was for the Cosmic Charity on behalf of the hospital's paediatric intensive-care unit.

A visit to Lahore, in Pakistan, to see her old friend Jemima Khan and husband Imran, brought out a selection of politically correct shalwar kameez—a blue and gold spot style; a turquoise and Delft blue print fabric, and another in turquoise and white floral print. There was also a Catherine Walker design in a soft, fondant pink.

That "something blue" cropped up yet again at a performance of the English National Ballet's *Swan Lake* in early June—a square-necked décolleté little high-summer shift

**EASTERN PROMISE** *(top, above, and right)* It was when Geeta Sarin, who designed for Rivaaz in Beauchamp Place (Jemima Khan also shops here), was awarded "Best Asian Designer of the Year" by the POW that the two struck up a rapport. One of Geeta's oufits for Diana was worn for her visit to London's Neasden Temple, on June 6, 1997. Designs for the Princess' shalwar kameez, worn largely on overseas trips, would be shared from then on between Sarin and Catherine Walker.

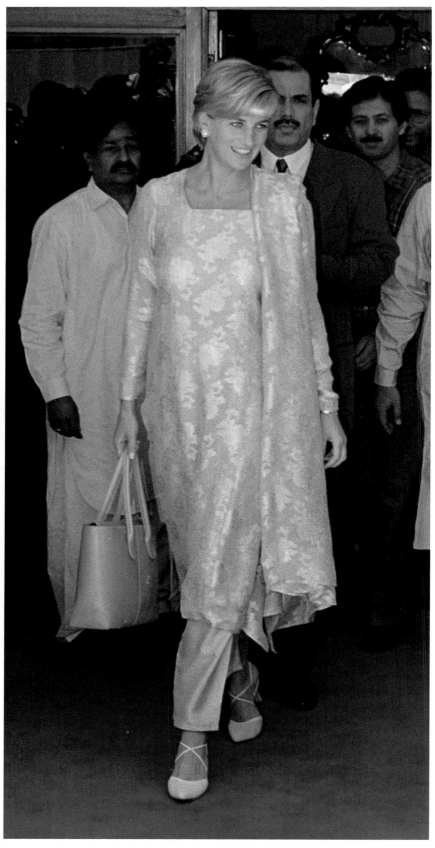

**PRINCE OF WALES CHECKS FOR A POW**
*(above)* A suitable choice for Diana's suit from
Galliano's début Dior couture collection that
sashayed down the runway in January of that
year. The Princess singled out this particular
checked suit with double-breasted, elongated
jacket with fringed detail, over a matching pencil
skirt (as well as optional trousers) from a video of
the show that was sent to her. The skirt version
was sighted in May 1997 on a visit to St Mary's
Hospital, London.

**BLUE BOMBSHELL** *(left)* "The Blue One and the
one that she wore on her 36th birthday—both my
evening dresses got the most press coverage of
any dresses at that time," boasts Azagury. It was
"The Blue One"—his little beaded décolletage-
defining number, with bow shoulder straps—that
the Princess wore to the ballet *Swan Lake* in June
1997; a veritable blue bombshell.

dress in pleated silk georgette, with teeny bows trimming the shoulder straps—a new Azagury design.

The high point of Diana's year was looming—her dress auction at Christie's New York salesrooms, an international event and a fashion "happening." In the run-up to auction day, there is a preview at Christie's in London, a party to which the designers are invited, together with the Princess and potential bidders.

Since the majority of dresses destined to go under the hammer are Catherine Walker designs—logical since the lady dominated Diana's wardrobe—it seems only right and proper that the Princess should pay homage to Walker by wearing her dresses to both the London party and the New York viewing preview.

Which, being politically correct, Diana does. And her dress code is short shifts. For the London reception, it is Walker's pale blue guipure lace-embroidered number; for across the

**JUST THE JOB** *(above)* Ronit Zilkha's cool, easy caramel-colored pants suit proved ideal for the flight and for arriving in the Big Apple.

**SEQUINS SAVE LIVES** *(right)* That was the theme of the auction, and Diana went along with the theme at Christie's New York preview.

## "I have never seen her so happy, particularly over those last three months."

JACQUES AZAGURY

Atlantic, another Walker shift-style, this time a short, glass-beaded one in a pastel pink and blue floral. Although she goes to the preview, Diana does not attend the New York auction in person. Perhaps the memories are too poignant, too painful—all those yesterdays under the hammer.

To travel to New York for the preview, Diana chooses a practical, caramel-colored, summer weight pants-suit by Ronit Zilkha. With a trendy headband on her hair, the Princess looks young and vital, the absolute epitome of the working woman of the late 1990s.

**BLUE FOR THE PREVIEW** *(left)* The Princess visits Christie's London saleroom for a preview of her dress auction in June 1997. To mark the occasion, and as a fitting tribute to favorite designer, Catherine Walker, whose dresses comprise the lion's share of the sale, Diana borrowed a pale blue, embroidered, crêpe guipure lace shift dress with a plunge-front.

**GLASS BEAD GAME** *(above)* Diana became ever more daring in her décolletage, and this pale gray, silk-scrolled, glass-bead-embroidered halter-necked dress, with sarong-style skirt, kept up the momentum. She had already set a precedent for wearing a sexy little number to London's Serpentine Gallery, and this 1995 choice, from Catherine Walker, was no exception. Lot No. 3 in the Christie's auction, it was bought by the Fashion Café for $77,300.

# The Christie's Sale

THERE ARE 79 LOTS in the Christie's New York auction "Dresses from the Collection of Diana, Princess of Wales"—50 by Catherine Walker, 11 Edelsteins, five Oldfields, three from Arbeid, two each from the Emanuels, Zandra Rhodes and Bellville-Sassoon/Lorcan Mullany; and one each from Hachi, Yuki, Gina Fratini, and Christina Stambolian.

The Gina Fratini white sari-style dress, designed whilst she was working at Norman Hartnell, went under the hammer for $85,000. Hachi's white one-shouldered glittering prize was bought by the *Daily Mail's "You"* magazine for $75,100, as the prize in a competition for their readers. And

**LOT NO. 71** *(above)* Worn to the first night of *Swan Lake* at the London Coliseum in 1989, Walker's high-busted, cream and salmon pink silk, slinky dinner-dress fetched $25,300.

**LOT NO. 1** *(top right)* "After shutting down in 1989, I went on and did a collection for Hartnell ... this was the last dress that I did for her, and the last time that I actually made a collection," says Gina Fratini. It was her stunning dress that opened the auction and got things off to a good start when this dress fetched $85,000.

**LOT NO. 53** *(bottom right)* Catherine Walker's enchanting coat-dress, which enjoyed a formal dinner at the Chateau de Chambord, France, in 1988, went under the hammer for $27,600.

**LOT NO. 46** *(opposite)* Photographed by Lord Snowdon for the Christie's auction catalogue, the Princess models Walker's ivory state dinner dress. It sold for $43,700.

Marsden Hospital Cancer Fund, AIDS Care Centre, New York Hospital-Cornell Medical Center, the Harvard AIDS Institute, and the Evelyn H. Lauder Breast Center of Memorial Sloan-Kettering Cancer Center.

Together with Liz Emanuel, Christina Stambolian, David Sassoon, and Lorcan Mullany, Zandra Rhodes was one of the few designers to attend the New York auction. Two of her water-colors of her own dresses appeared in the auction catalogue.

"I had thought about buying my dresses back, but I hadn't got that sort of money, as I am trying to raise funds to build my museum in London," says Zandra.

## "She fitted in totally with her wonderful image."

ZANDRA RHODES

Stambolian's wicked little black so-called "Divorce" dress fetched $74,000. But it was Edelstein's midnight velvet "Travolta" dress that hit the jackpot, reaching the princessly sum of $222,500.

A letter from the Princess, dated June 1997, reads: "The inspiration for this wonderful sale comes from just one person ... our son William."

The auction raised a grand total of $3,258,750. Proceeds from the sale, as well as from the catalogue sales, went to AIDS Crisis Trust, London's Royal

"I suppose it must have been 1983 or 1984 when I first met Princess Diana," recalls Zandra. "She fitted in totally with her wonderful image. She was like a fairytale princess."

Chanel designer, Karl Lagerfeld recalls, "She had never looked so good, so fashionable, as in the last six months. I think that she finally felt more free ... free from that stiff English fashion."

And in the words of Jacques Azagury, "I have never seen her so happy, particularly over those last

**LOT NO. 27** *(above)* This Catherine Walker creation was bought by the Instituto Zuzu Angel for a museum in Rio de Janeiro for $51,750.

**LOT NO. 5** *(right)* First seen on an official trip to Thailand in 1988, this sari-style dress, also by Ms Walker, went under the hammer for $48,300.

three months. I was dealing with her a lot, seeing her almost every day at the time. You could tell that she was a happy woman; it was oozing out of her, and she looked so fit."

Robina Ziff recalls: "The last time that I saw her was at Harry's Bar on July 9. She was wearing a white suit, and she looked absolutely wonderful. I said to the girls at Escada: 'I have never seen her looking so radiant.'"

*large stone.*

*size of pearls at points on hem & base of shoulder frill.*

*diamonds in pink. to put glitter into squares at hem.*

*ZandraRhodes*
*style 85/54*

**THE PRINCESS ... PRETTY IN PINK** *(above)*
It was sister-in-law Fergie, who was a Zandra aficionado, who introduced Diana to the zany designer. A flashback to 1986 sees the POW wearing this dress to a State Banquet in Kyoto, during her official visit to Japan. It has Rhodes' signature kerchief-style, pointed hemline, and the off-the-shoulder neckline is not dissimilar to David Sassoon's "Gonzaga" dress. Zandra's original sketch *(left)* for this fairy-tale dress illustrates the fabric detail in close-up, as well as the embroidery, and the pearls and glass beads, trimmed in paste, that form patterns of lozenges and circles. As Lot No. 47, the dress went under the auctioneer's hammer for $27,600.

# England's Rose

**PURELY PRACTICAL** *(above)* For Bosnia, as in Angola, Diana dressed in an easy, relaxed, laid-back way, to enable her to concentrate on the issue, rather than concerning herself with clothes.

**DIANA AND DODI** *(right)* It was all speculative—what might have been, could have been, we will never know, but at least the Princess knew some happiness in the last few days of her life.

**INDIAN ROSE** *(opposite)* "In the fairy tale, it's important what the Princess wears, but with Diana it was her personality that was important, and that's what fashion should be," believes designer Ann Demeulemeester.

AT JUST TURNED 36, the Princess was still a young, beautiful cover-girl. There was every chance of her finding personal happiness and maybe even extending her family, bearing a much-desired daughter.

On July 22, Diana attended the memorial service of her close friend Gianni Versace, assassinated outside his home in Miami. Dressed in one of his sleeveless short shift-dresses, she sat in church with their mutual friend, Elton John, whom she comforted and consoled. Little did he know that in just over a month's time he would be writing the lyrics for a song to her that would make the whole world weep.

Her trip to Bosnia in early August was, sadly, the last such mercy mission she would make, but the knock-on effect of her intervention would be far-reaching and would help to focus the minds and actions of politicians.

In late August she is in the South of France with Mohammad Al Fayed's son, Dodi, for a short break on his father's boat in the Mediterranean. The pair have a great time in St Tropez, but their relationship, whatever it was or might have been, was short-lived. The rest, as they say, is history.

In the early hours of the morning of August 31, 1997, the world said goodbye to England's Rose. Overnight Diana was no more, but through her efforts, she left the world a better place.

Victor Edelstein believes: "Diana and Evita (Eva Peron) are the two women of this century who had this incredible rapport with the people—a nation going mad over a young, blonde, beautiful woman, who took an interest in the poor." Loved, worshipped, adored—Diana was certainly all of these.

As it transpired, the Christie's auction was a master-stroke, linking the Princess' work, her passion for fashion, and also her humanitarian qualities. In auctioning off those dresses, she left a global legacy. And, because of her untimely death, these dresses continue to give tremendous pleasure and, most importantly, to raise money for worthwhile charities.

The anthem "I vow to thee my country" had been her own choice for her wedding. She had stuck by it. Diana was a diamond of impeccable cut, color, and clarity. The brilliant will continue to shine.

"She was such a lovely, dear girl. She had enthusiasm, fun; you couldn't help but love her; she always made you feel so special," remembers Gina Fratini.

"She had the most amazing effect on this world. I think that her death will change this country for the better, and that was her life-long wish. It is tragic that she had to die for it; please God that we appreciate what she did, and that she did not die in vain.

"This is the way that she could contribute to the world, and to this country. Don't let's ever forget what she did for this country," says Gina, wistfully. "She would have made the most wonderful Queen."

Which, in her way, she was. Initially, the POW was regarded as the Queen of Fashion, but as she grew, both in style and stature, she transcended clothes. Diana was also the Queen of Hearts.

The Princess had grown into something of a Younger States-woman; she would prove the making of the modern British monarchy.

England's Rose blossomed and flourished. No-one could ever have envisaged that she would disappear from our garden whilst still in full bloom, to be remembered as forever young. She was cut down in her prime, but from that single Super-Rosa grew a magic carpet of flowers, a tribute the likes of which the world had never seen.

Where have all the flowers gone? Gone to Diana, every one.

# Index and Acknowledgements

**PICTURE CREDITS**

Alpha Photographic Press: 15, 16, 17, 21, 22, 23, 24, 28, 29, 31, 32, 33, 34, 35, 36, 37, 38, 39, 40, 41, 42, 44, 45, 46, 47, 48, 49, 50, 51, 52, 53, 54, 55, 56, 57, 60, 61, 64, 65, 66, 67, 69, 70, 71, 72, 73, 74, 75, 76, 77, 78, 79, 80, 82, 84, 85, 89, 90, 91, 92, 93, 96, 97, 98, 99, 100, 101, 102, 103, 104, 105, 106, 107, 119, 121, 122, 123, 135, 136, 137, 138, 140, 141, 142.
Anwar Hussein; 9, 25, 34, 40, 54, 58, 65, 67, 72, 76, 89, 105, 115.
Big Pictures: 143.
Camera Press: 5, 12, 13, 15, 18, 19, 20, 21, 22, 26, 30, 32, 33, 38, 39, 45, 46, 52, 54, 55, 68, 74, 77, 83, 86, 87, 88, 120, 139, 143.
Conde Nast: 14, 92, 113.
Ben Costa: 122.
Nunn Syndication: 71.
Neils Obee: 108.
Photographers International: 11 right.
Press Association; 10, 73, 97, 100, 109, 120, 123, 127, 128, 132, 137.
Rex Features: 11 left, 27, 83.
Universal Pictorial Press: 56.

All other pictures are from private collections.

**JACKIE MODLINGER**

I would like to thank the fashion designers featured in this book for all their help, as well as Mary Flack of Fenwick in New Bond Street, Robina Ziff of Escada, and Simon Wilson of Butler and Wilson. Thanks also to my long-suffering husband, Ben, and to my sister Madeleine Kingsley, who helped me through the creation of this book.